D1824672

PENGUIN BOOKS

The Penguin Folk Guitar Manual

John Pearse, an offspring of the 1950s guitar revolution, was born
in 1939 and spent his early boyhood in Wales bemoaning the fact
that his hand wasn't big enough to hold down an F chord. Guitarist,
guitar maker, teacher and writer of everything from songs to guitar
manuals to children's stories, he was approached by the BBC in
London in 1964 to write and present 'Hold Down a Chord', the
first series of guitar lessons to be televised. A second series, 'Finger-
picking', followed in 1968, and since then millions have learned
to play from showings of these now-legendary programmes in
Germany, Australia, New Zealand and Canada.

John Pearse now resides in London with his two basset hounds and
other friends, and does frequent concert tours in Europe and
America. He is the author of more than thirty guitar books, including
the mammoth 'Guitarist's Picture Chord Encyclopedia'.

The Penguin Folk Guitar Manual

John Pearse

PENGUIN BOOKS

Penguin Books Ltd, Harmondsworth, Middlesex, England
Penguin Books, 625 Madison Avenue, New York, New York 10022, U.S.A.
Penguin Books Australia Ltd, Ringwood, Victoria, Australia
Penguin Books Canada Ltd, 2801 John Street, Markham, Ontario,
Canada L3R 1B4
Penguin Books (N.Z.) Ltd, 182–190 Wairau Road, Auckland 10, New Zealand

First published in the United States of America under the title 'Frets and Fingers'
by Paddington Press 1978
First published in Great Britain under the title 'Frets and Fingers'
by Paddington Press 1978
Published in Penguin Books 1979

Made and printed in Great Britain by
Butler & Tanner Ltd, Frome and London
Set in Century Schoolbook

CONTENTS

Since its introduction into the United States, the guitar has undergone many swings of fashion. Initially a parlor instrument for the ladies of quality, it was carried along the trails west, in the Conestoga wagons of the pioneering settlers, and went with the paddle steamers along the waterways as far south as New Orleans. It even ended up in the Klondike, carried there on muleback by the prospectors in 1849.

In short, the guitar became the classless instrument of a new country, a country which drew its strength and traditions from those of Europe and Africa. It was the instrument of the preacher and the prostitute, the slave and the Southern belle. As America grew, the independent spirit of its society was reflected in both the instrument and its music. Established musical patterns were tried first, of course; but if they no longer fit, they were set aside and something new was developed. The guitar, too, was modified by the society. It was enlarged, braced in new ways, and finally even equipped with metal strings.

Perhaps the greatest innovator was a young immigrant from Markneukirchen in Saxony, who came to America in the early 1800s, looking for the freedom to practice his chosen profession of guitar maker. That man was Christian Frederick Martin—and it is to him, and his descendants, that this book is respectfully dedicated.

John Pearse
London, 1978

ACKNOWLEDGMENTS

A book of this scope could not have been attempted without the support and encouragement of my friends. My thanks go out to everyone who allowed me to talk *at* them during the gestation period, and who offered many helpful suggestions. In particular I should like to thank Michael Grey-Jones for the really beautiful illustrations which he did so painstakingly, time after time until they showed exactly what we needed. Thanks, too, to Tom and Mary Anne Evans for taking precious time off from the writing of their mammoth history of the guitar to "jolly me along" at a time when nothing seemed to be going right. Tom, by the way, shot all the guide photographs from which Michael drew the hand positions.

Grateful thanks also to the Paddington Design Department: particularly to Patricia Pillay, designer; Eileen Batterberry, who hand-set each of the tablature staves and chord windows; and Henry Sunderland, who with the help of Jernome the Gnome burned the midnight Fosters to perfect the layout.

And to my editor, Diane "Absolutely perfect. Couldn't be better. There's just one small change . . ." Flanel, the soul of diplomacy. I shouldn't forget the bassets either, Hercules and The Gimp, who ensured that not only did I get sufficient exercise but caused me to develop such skill as a carpet shampooer that, should the guitar ever go out of favor, I have another string to my bow. Lastly, my thanks to Val for continuing to live with me throughout the writing of the book, and then offering to type out the final draft. Such bravery should not go unnoticed!

PREFACE

Although Necessity may occasionally be the mother of invention, for me at least Frustration has been a much more likely candidate. As a small boy in Wales, right at the start of the early '50s guitar "boom," I trudged around the music stores in search of a guitar manual which would teach me how to play my newly acquired guitar—only to find that every book seemed to be written for use by a guitar teacher. Not much help to a beginner having to go it on his own!

As time went by I discovered, deduced, stumbled across tips, strums and other haphazard bits of guitar "lore," much in the same way that an untrained archeology buff might sift through topsoil looking for shards and fragments, but never too sure what they are or how they might fit together. All this time I was still compulsively buying every new "How To" book that appeared in my local music store—and just as quickly discarding it as, yet again, it didn't fulfill its stated intention: to teach me how to play the guitar!

Luckily, by the time I was seventeen, I had begun to meet up with other guitar nuts, both amateur and professional, and they showed me where I was going wrong and provided that overall framework which made all my own discoveries fall into place—something that no book had ever done for me.

I suppose that the seeds of my own guitar-teaching method were planted around this time.

Obviously the best way to learn an instrument is to go to a teacher —but for the majority of people, this just isn't practical. There may not be a good teacher in the neighborhood—or, if there is, it's often not possible to get along there for regular lessons. Many teachers, too, seem to cling to outmoded methods, teaching by repetition and making the learning of the guitar a drudge rather than an exciting experience.

Why, I wondered, hadn't someone developed a planned teaching method which showed how easy it was to play the guitar, which explained simply and in everyday language the framework, or "grammar," of guitar playing?

A method that didn't force newcomers to learn standard music notation at the same time as they were trying to come to terms with the involved finger movements of guitar playing.

A method based on the simplest form of written music: tablature, with a line for each string of the guitar and numbers marked on those string lines to show exactly where the notes should be played.

A really foolproof method that moved smoothly and effortlessly through all the basic structures of traditional guitar technique.

A method, moreover, that gave constant reinforcement to the most unconfident student, providing continuous proof of his or her developing expertise.

In short, a method which not only removed the need for a teacher but also stripped away the fusty traditions of guitar teaching and showed students just how easy—really easy—it was to learn to play the guitar.

It had to be possible.

In the early '60s I began to put my theories to the test, running a weekly guitar class for the English Folk Dance and Song Society. By 1964 I had classes all over London running every night of the week and in the fall of the following year the BBC commissioned me to write and present the first-ever series of televised guitar lessons. The success of this series, "Hold Down a Chord," kept me very busy writing follow-up books—on Ragtime, Blues and so on—but I never lost the nagging feeling that I still hadn't licked the basic problem of teaching "at a distance."

Sure, if people came to my lessons—or if they followed the TV course—they could learn guitar. But what if they couldn't come, or if the TV show wasn't on in their area? The books could be used on their own, letters coming in from all over showed that most people were getting on fine. Most people—but not everyone. There were other letters, too. Letters from people who needed a different kind of book. The kind of book for which I'd hunted when first I got a guitar.

I became so dissatisfied with the situation that I decided that I couldn't put it off any longer. That book had to be written. It took two years. Two years of sitting with students watching just how they worked through the books they were using. Two years of developing a new tablature form that was not only clearer to read and understand—but which also *looked* clearer. Two years of trial and error, of blind alleys and breakthroughs; of locating pitfalls and removing them.

Well, here it is.

It's a complete course covering everything that you'll need to know as you transform yourself into a guitar player. Even if you are someone who has been playing for years you will find something here for you. Something to make you sit back and say, "Aha! So that's how it's done."

Start right at the very beginning and work your way through. Don't skip anything—even if you think that you already know it, or that it's kid's stuff. You'll be surprised!

Just how long it will take you to get to the end of the book depends on you. If you're a professional just brushing up on technique, you'll do it in a couple of weeks (any quicker and you're just not using the book properly). If you're a beginner, it will take you considerably longer—but I promise that you'll be playing melodies painlessly in only a few weeks. And when you finally close the book and put it away on your bookshelf, you'll be a guitarist!

Happy playing.

WHY A GUITAR WORKS

Before I start to show you how to play the guitar, it might be helpful if we take a look at the instrument.

Although it looks a fairly complex beast, the principles that enable a guitar to make music are very basic and easy to understand.

When you were at school, I'm sure that you trapped the end of a ruler under the closed lid of your desk and "twunked" it with your thumb.

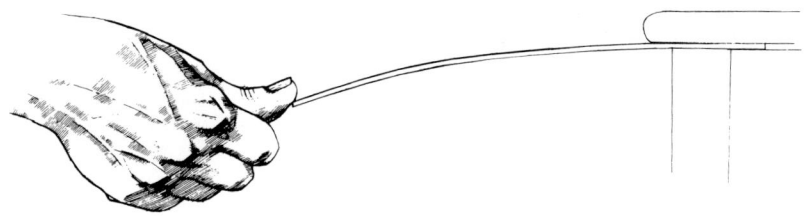

The note you heard was produced by the ruler vibrating, and the loudness of the note was due to the desk "taking up" the vibrations via the trapped end.

You also must have noticed that if you pushed the ruler further into the desk, so that the amount that you could twunk on was reduced,

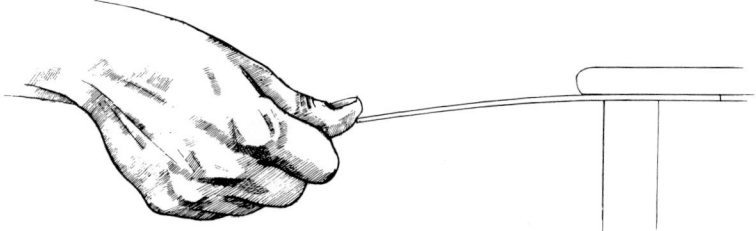

then the pitch of the note which was produced was higher.

The shorter the vibrating length, the higher the note.

The longer the vibrating length, the lower the note.

Now, if instead of a ruler you trapped the end of a piece of string inside the desk, pulled it reasonably taut and then plucked it, again you'd get a note.

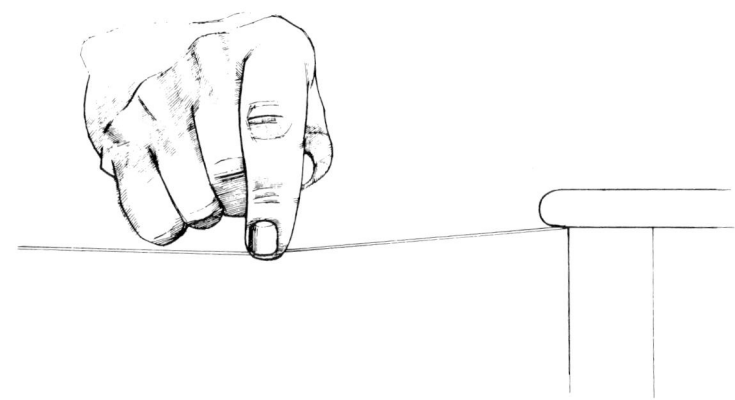

If you shortened the string slightly, you would find that the pitch of the note would rise. If you lengthened it, however, the note would fall—just like the notes produced by the ruler.

But you probably noticed something else.

If you *pulled harder* on the string, the pitch of the note would rise.

If, on the other hand, you *relaxed* the tension slightly, then the note would drop in pitch.

So, unlike the ruler, it was possible to change the pitch of a string note in *two* ways:

    1. By lengthening or shortening the string

      and

    2. By tightening or slackening it.

In both cases the sound was "amplified" by the hollow desk.
It is these simple principles that enable a guitar to work.

When a guitar string is plucked, it vibrates and a note is produced.
At one end, the string passes over the BRIDGE SADDLE,

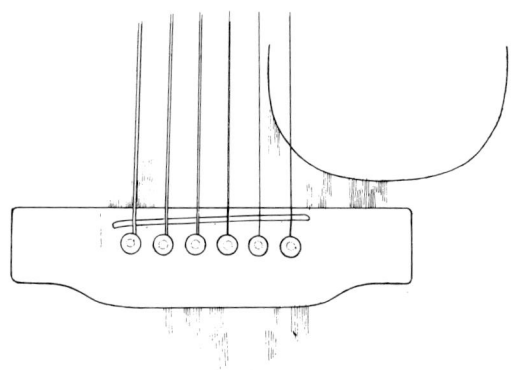

which transmits the vibrations efficiently to the TABLE—or BELLY—
of the guitar.

This table is braced on the inside in such a way that it is *strong*
enough to withstand the combined pull of all six strings without
being damaged, and yet *flexible* enough to vibrate when the string
vibrations are passed to it by the bridge.

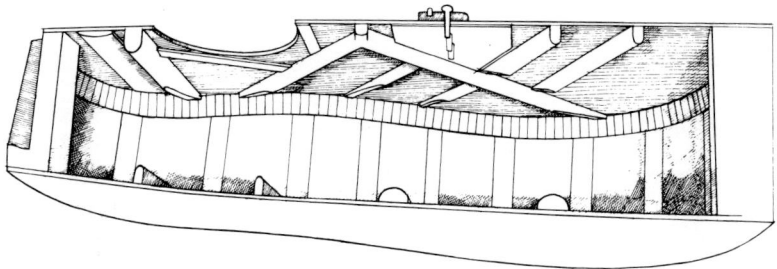

This fine balance between strength and flexibility is very critical.

If the table is not strong enough, then the pull of the strings will cause it to swell and maybe even shatter!

If the table is too rigid, then the guitar will not have a good, sonorous tone.

As the string vibrations pass through the table, they cause the air within the body of the guitar to vibrate as well. This has the effect of intensifying and amplifying the sound, just like the hollow desk amplified the ruler.

The other end of the string is attached to a TUNING PEG at the head of the guitar.

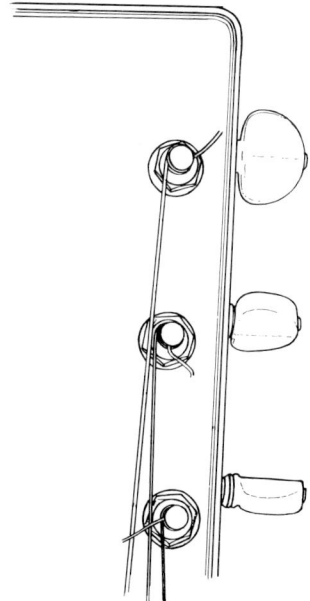

This is rather like a small capstan, the barrel of which is rotated by the turning of a small button.

As this capstan turns, it winds the string around itself, stretching it with increasing tension.

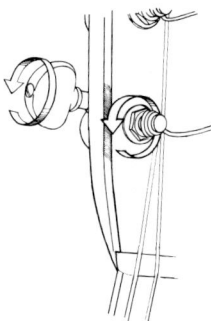

As you discovered with the string and the desk experiment, this increase in tension causes the pitch of the string to rise, and so it is by means of this stretching principle that the string is raised in pitch to "tune" it for playing.

Between the peghead and bridge, the string passes over the FINGERBOARD.

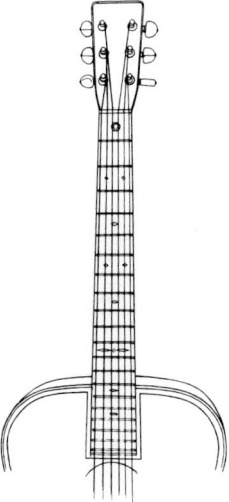

This is a hardwood strip—usually rosewood or ebony—which runs along the neck of the instrument. It is divided into sections by the FRET BARS, which are inlaid into it.

You remember that shortening the vibrating length of both the ruler and the string caused the pitch of the note to rise?

Well, the frets are used for just this purpose.

If you push down a string just behind a fret and then pluck it, the vibrating length of the string is reduced—and the pitch is raised.

Simple, isn't it?

These, then, are the basic principles upon which a guitar works:

If a string is *shortened*, the note it produces is *raised*.

If a string is *lengthened*, the note it produces is *lowered*.

If a string is *tautened*, the note it produces is *raised*.

If a string is *slackened*, the note it produces is *lowered*.

PUTTING STRINGS ON YOUR GUITAR

What strings you use on your guitar depends upon what type of guitar you have.

If you have a traditional CLASSIC guitar with a wide, flat fingerboard and Spanish-style loop bridge,

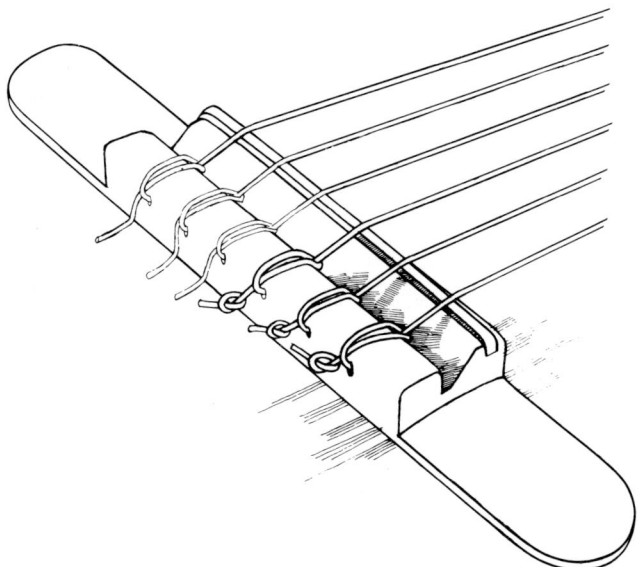

then you *must* use string sets which are nylon based.

These have three light strings—the treble strings—made of nylon which has been extruded in a long thread or filament, and three heavy strings which are made by winding a soft metal wire around a core of hair-fine nylon filaments. These are the bass strings.

Strings of this type have been
developed by generations of guitar
makers and players to produce the
best possible sound from the lightly
made classic guitar. ▶

◀ If, on the other hand, you have
a modern FLAT-TOP or JUMBO style
guitar, with a narrow, curved
fingerboard and pinned bridge,

then the best tonal results can only be obtained if you use string sets which are metal based.

These have three light treble strings which are made of plain polished steel wire, and three bass strings which are made by winding a soft metal wire around a steel wire core.

These strings exert a much greater strain on the body of a guitar than do those which are nylon based, and for this reason must *never ever* be used to string a classic-type instrument. To do so would certainly cause the neck to warp and deform the lightly braced table! On a guitar built to withstand their pull, however, they produce a rich tone of great volume.

Here is how you should string both kinds of guitar.

THE CLASSIC GUITAR

We'll start with the *sixth* string.

That's the thickest one.

Take the string out of its packet and carefully unroll it.

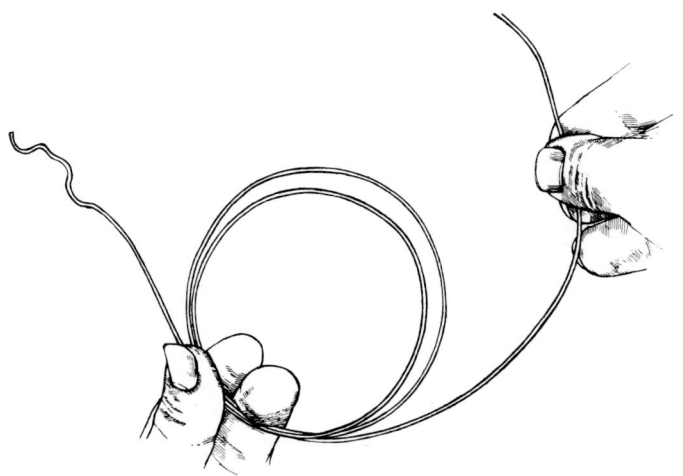

This may seem a very obvious thing to say, but the important word is CAREFULLY!

As I told you, the string is made by winding a *soft* metal wire onto a filament core—so rough handling of the string can easily damage it.

If the winding gets kinked, then the string won't vibrate evenly and the tone will suffer. Careless unrolling can loosen the bond between the winding and core. Should this happen the string will either buzz or sound so muffled as to be quite useless.

So take care!

Right! When you've unrolled the string you will see that one end of it (at the left of the illustration) is very soft and pliable.

This allows the string to bend easily, enabling it to be secured at the bridge.

Lay the guitar face up across your knees and thread the string through the sixth string hole in the bridge.

Thread from *behind* the bridge, using the *rigid* string end.

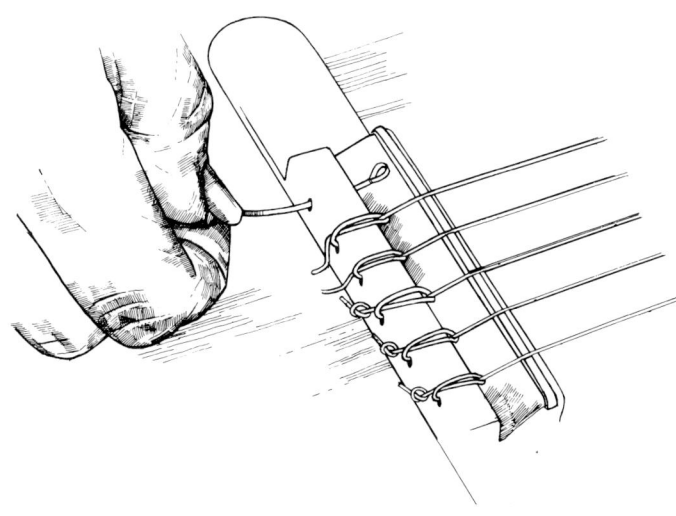

Now, gently, pull the string through until just the pliable section of string remains behind the bridge.

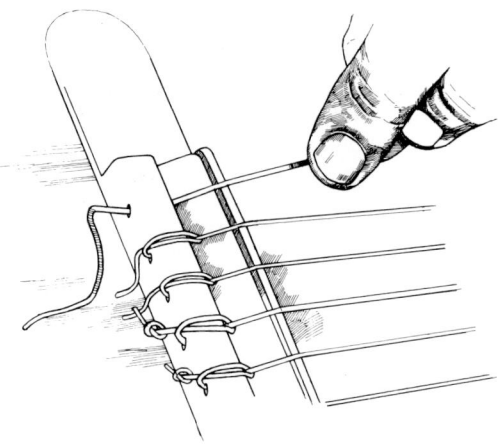

OK?

Right! Now bring this pliable section *up across* the top of the bridge . . .

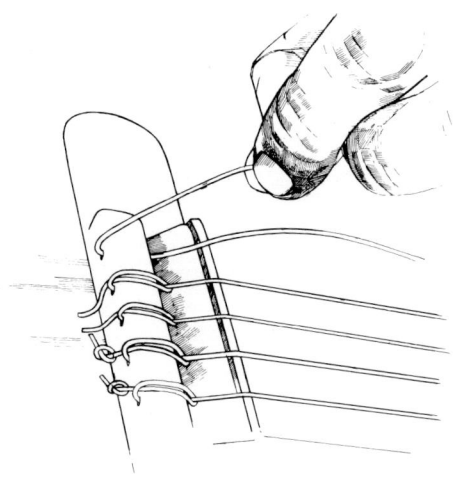

and pass it *under* the string.

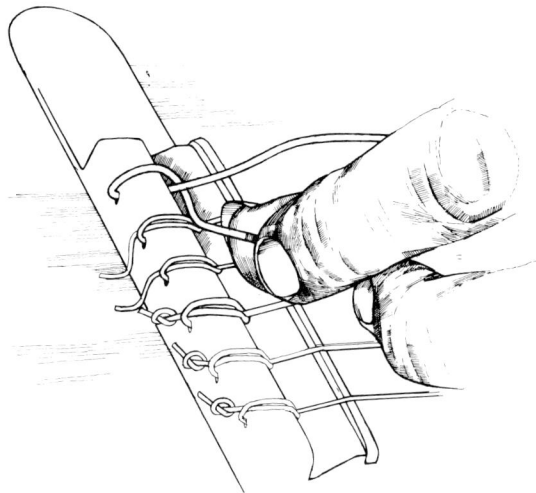

Lead it back and pass it *under* itself.

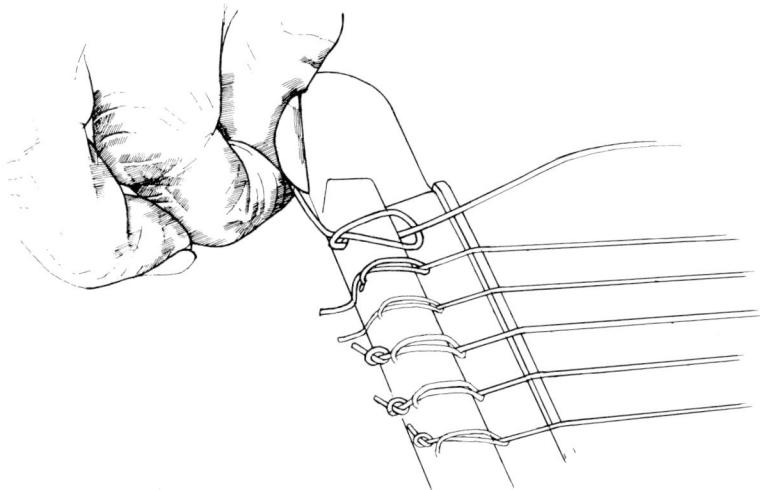

Finally, pull the very end down *behind* the bridge.

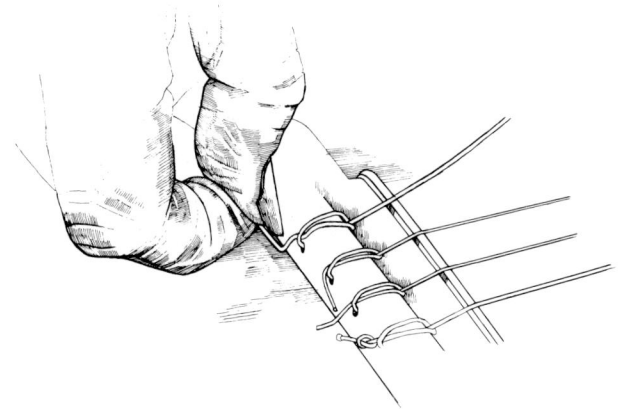

To tighten the fixing, *gently* pull the string in front of the bridge.

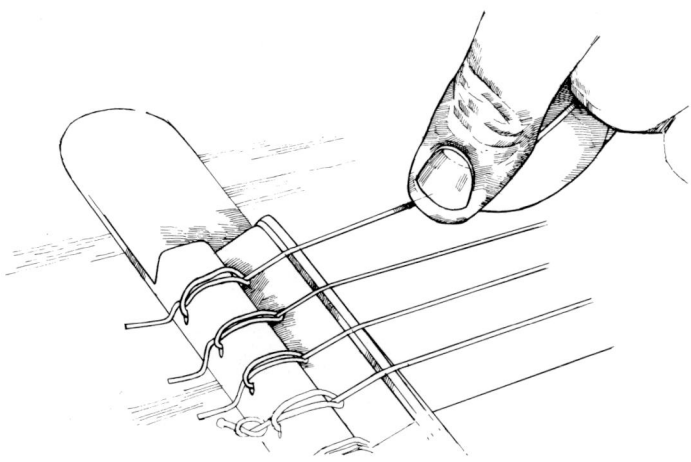

How did you get on?

Not so hard, is it?

If you find that the fixing isn't holding firm, don't worry. Take the string off and try again. Like most things, it's a knack.

Now to the other end of the guitar.

Take hold of the rigid string end and lead it, gently, along the length of the guitar until you get to the peg head.

Still with the guitar across your knees, turn the button which operates the sixth tuner to rotate the winding barrel.

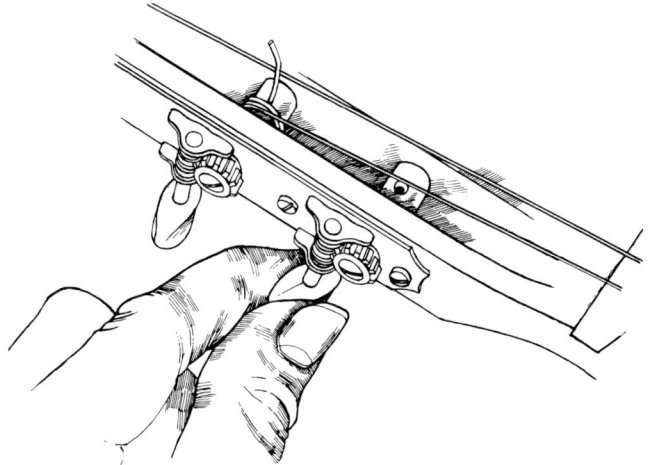

Keep turning until the string-holding hole is facing you.

Now thread the string *through* the barrel . . .

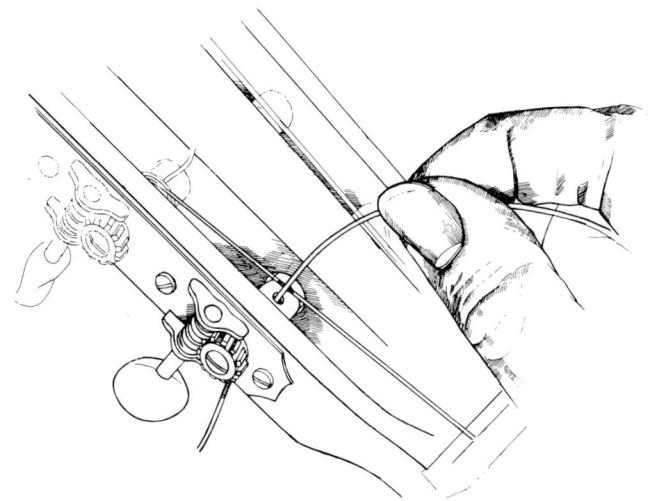

and lead the end *around* and *under* itself.

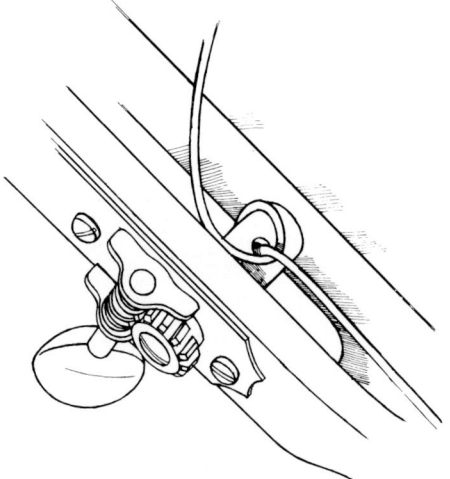

This will bind and hold the string firm when you tune it.

Now, with your right hand, grasp the string between the head and the end of the fingerboard . . . and hold it away from the instrument, taking up the slack.

With your left hand, begin to wind the string onto the barrel, using your right hand to guide the coils and keep an even tension.

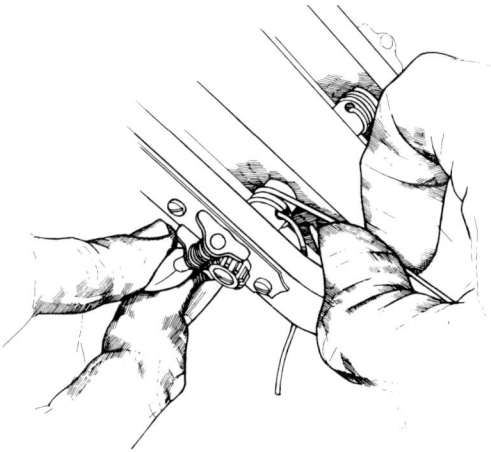

As you wind, make sure that the string does not stack against the side of the head slot, as this can deform the winding and weaken the string.

Take your time and relax.

If things start to go adrift, just unwind and start again.

Remember, besides looking good, a well-stacked string will play better and last longer.

So take your time.

When the last of the slack has been taken up, unroll the fifth string and put that on; then the fourth.

As I told you earlier, the three treble strings of your guitar are not wound. This means that a little more care must be taken when attaching them at the bridge end, or they just might slip free.

Since I started you off on the sixth string, by the time you get to string number three you should have just about mastered the art of bridge fixing—so an unwound string shouldn't prove too daunting.

Here is the best way I've come across to attach it firmly.

First, tie a simple knot right at one end of the string.

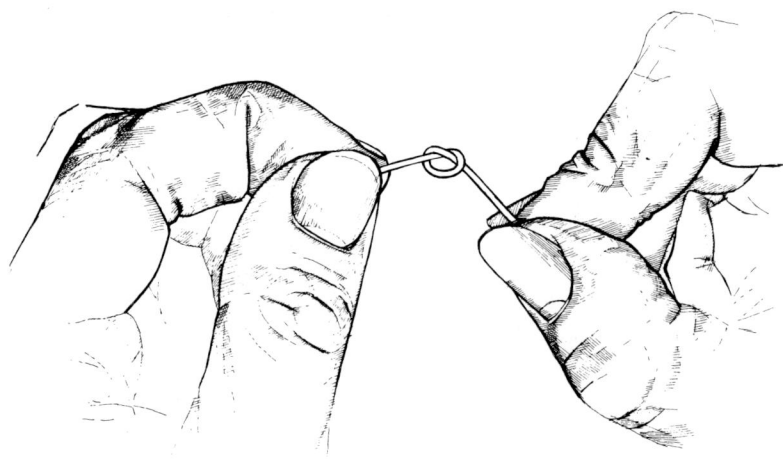

As there's no winding, there's no pliable end—so the knot can be tied at either end.   OK?

Now, thread the *unknotted* end through the hole in the bridge, from back to front, leaving about 2 inches—and the knot—behind the bridge.

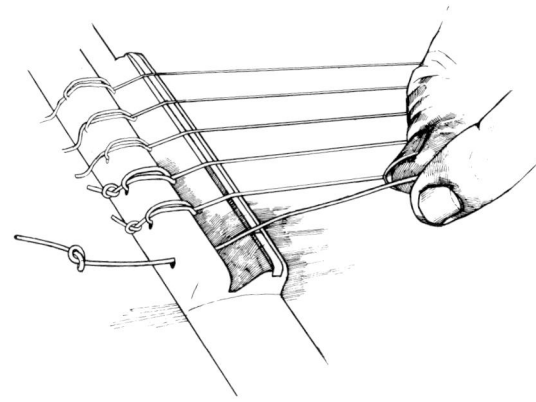

How's it coming?

As with the wound strings, lead the end of the string *over* the top of the bridge and pass it *under* itself.

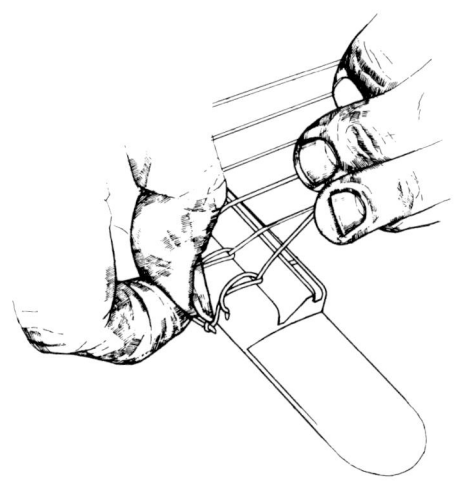

Finally, pull the knot down *behind* the bridge.

Now, *gently,* pull on the string in front of the bridge in order to tighten the fixing.

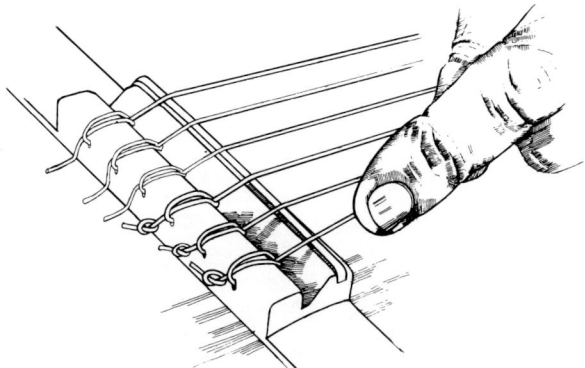

You're now ready to attach the free end to the tuner.

So much for a classic guitar.

What about the flat-top guitar and metal-based strings?

THE FLAT-TOP GUITAR

Well, the most popular bridge design for this type of guitar employs
a system known as PINNING.

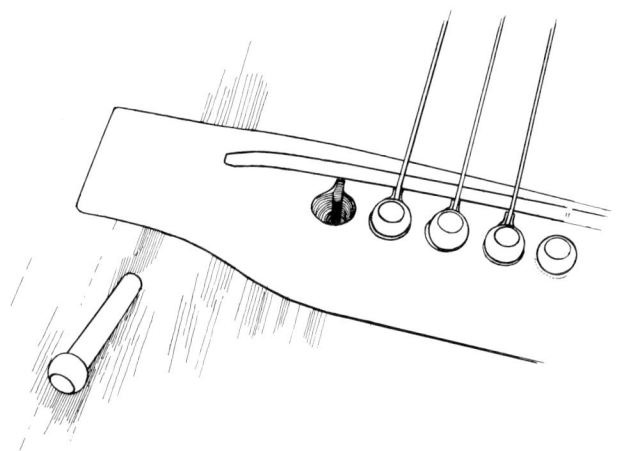

In a pinned bridge, the string ends are poked into the body of the
guitar through vertical holes in the bridge, and secured in place by
means of small tapered plugs (or pins) of wood, ivory or plastic.

This style of bridge construction is actually fairly ancient and can
be seen on many gut-strung guitars made in Germany in the early
1800s. Legend has it that it was taken to America by Christian
Frederick Martin, a German guitar maker who settled there in the
1830s and whose family guitar firm is credited with building the
first metal-strung flat-top guitars in the 1900s.

Here's how to put strings on a pinned-bridge guitar.

As with the classic guitar, we start by unrolling the sixth string.

As before, be gentle—and also take care as the string unrolls. A
metal sixth string is very "whippy" and can unroll with the agility
of a striking snake . . . so watch out for your eyes!

When you've got it unrolled, you'll see that one end has a small
metal bobbin attached.

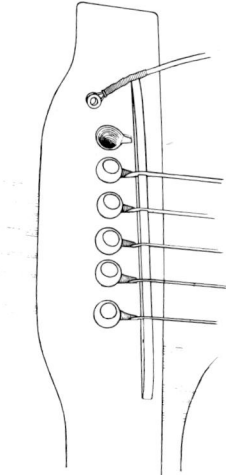

This is known as the BALL, and such a string is known as a BALL-END STRING.

Some years ago you had a choice. You could buy either ball-end or loop-end strings for metal-strung guitars. Now, like so many things, the loop-ends have vanished.

So, you've taken the string from its packet and unrolled it.

Lay the guitar face up on your knees . . .

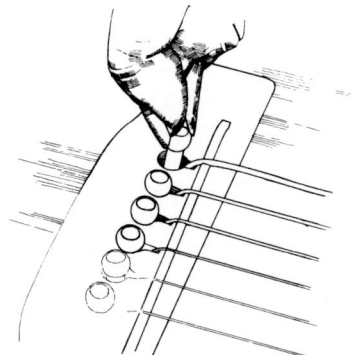

and, with finger and thumb, try to pull out the sixth bridge pin.

IMPORTANT: Don't *ever* remove a bridge pin which is securing a string until you have slackened off the string tension *completely*.

Now, sometimes a pin will pop out with no trouble. More often than not, however, it will need slight persuasion. One tried and true method is to lever against the underside of the pin head with a coin.

This has to be done carefully so it doesn't deform the pin or scratch the surface of the bridge.

I actually prefer the following technique for releasing a stubborn bridge pin—but again, it must be done *carefully*!

Hook the edge of the coin under the pin head and, using the next pin as a fulcrum or pivot, *gently* rock the coin to exert pressure. The pin should then pop out.

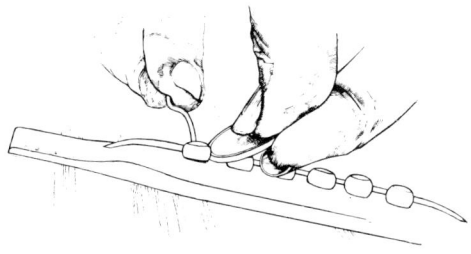

Occasionally, you will encounter one which is really impacted and which would break rather than be budged by levering.

In such a case, put your hand into the body of the guitar through the soundhole and—*gently*—push up on the pin from the inside.

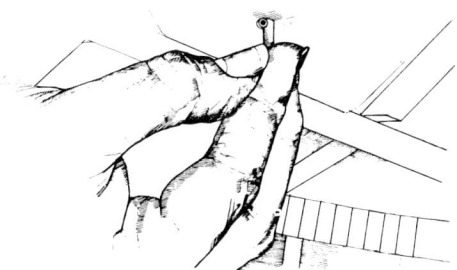

If it's still jammed tight, using a small hard object about the size of a cigarette lighter, give a couple of sharp taps on the pin from the inside of the guitar.

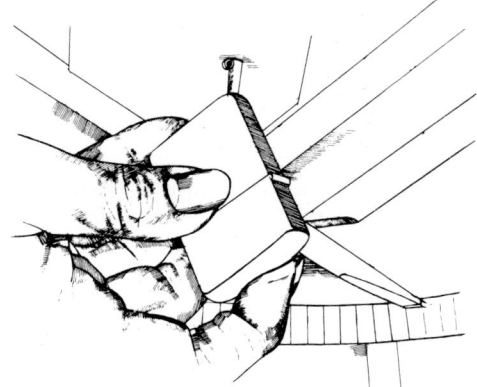

This will loosen the most stubborn of pins, but should only be used as a last resort.

Once the pin is out, the ball end of your sixth string should be fed through the hole to a depth of approximately 1 inch. The pin should then be replaced in such a way that the string emerges from the side of the pin hole toward the peg head.

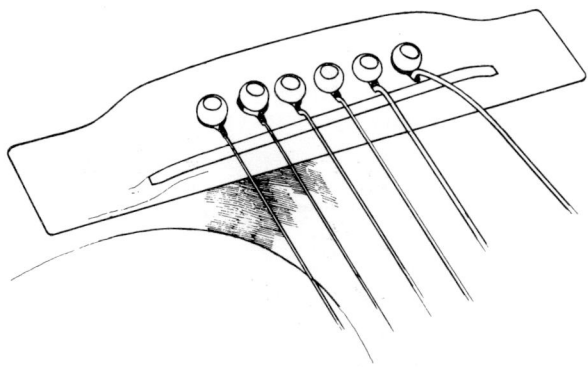

Many bridge pins have a groove running down one side.

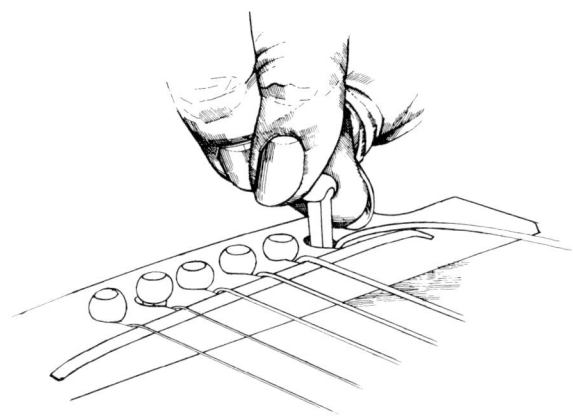

This is to enclose the string just above the ball, and so a pin of this type should be inserted with this groove also facing toward the peg head.

Having replaced the bridge pin, hold it in firmly while pulling gently on the free end of the string to "lock" the ball under the bridge. As with nylon-based strings, you should be as gentle as possible when dealing with metal-based strings.

Now, lead the free end of the string along the length of the guitar— and you are ready to affix it at the peg head.

Some flat-top-style guitars have a classic-type slotted peg head.

If yours is one that has, simply attach the string in exactly the same way that you would a nylon-based string.

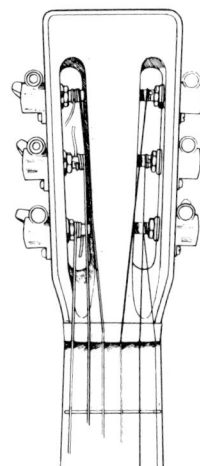

If, on the other hand, the guitar has
a flat "spade" head, with the tuner
barrels poking through from behind,
then the procedure is slightly different.

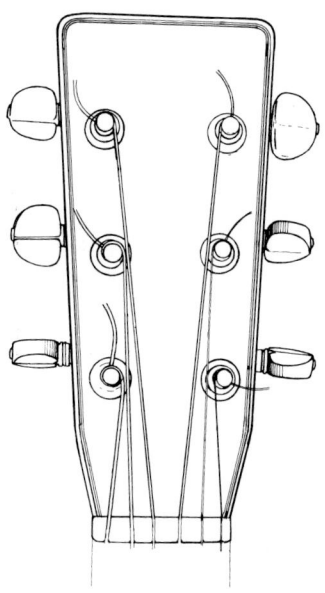

Hold the guitar on your knee as if you were about to play it.

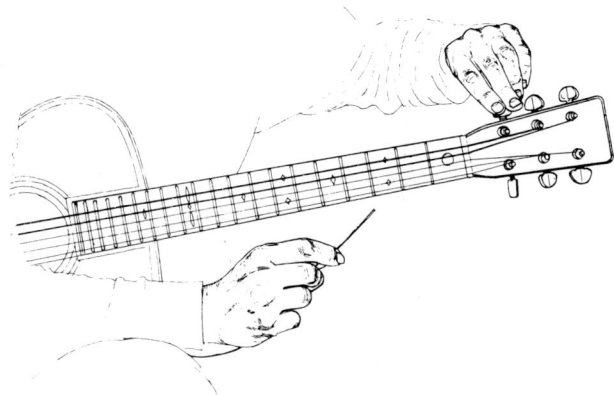

Then turn the sixth-string peg button, rotating the barrel to bring
the string hole uppermost.

Now, thread the string from the inside of the head out toward you,

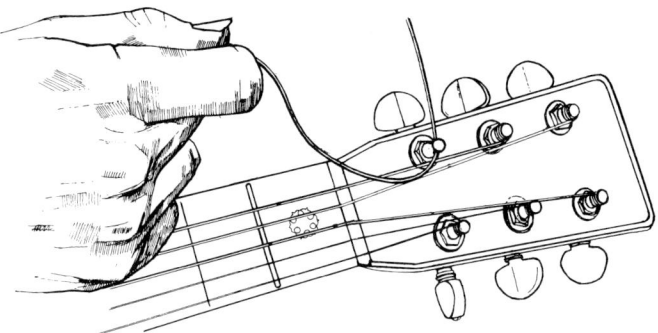

double it back on itself,

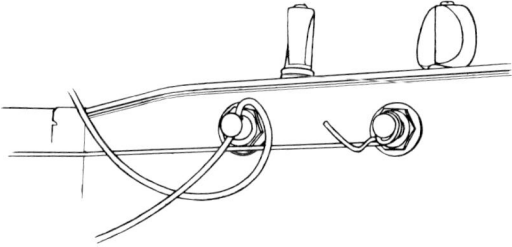

and pull the end gently outward.

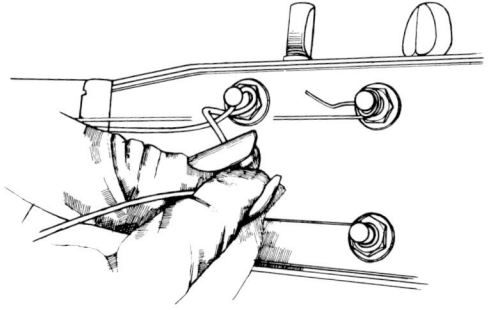

Taking up the slack with your right hand, slowly wind the slack onto the barrel, using your right hand to ensure that the string stacks evenly from the *top* to the *bottom* of the barrel.

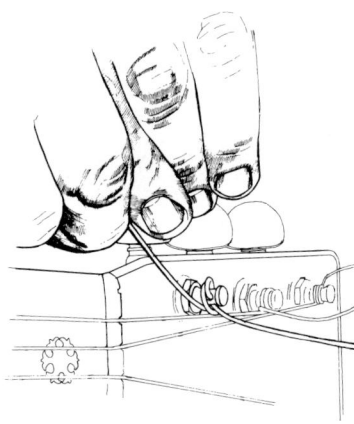

All the other strings, including the unwound trebles, are dealt with in the same way.

DEALING WITH UNTIDY STRING ENDS

Before you cut any wound string, you must kink it about 1 inch beyond its exit from the barrel.

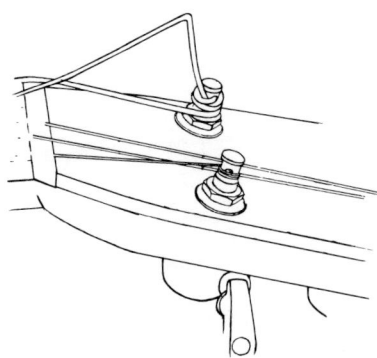

This is to guard against any possible loosening of the winding on the core which, as you now know, can cause buzzing or loss of tone.

You can then cut off the string end just past this point.

Although an unwound string obviously doesn't need to be kinked, it *is* a good idea to allow about 1 inch or so between the barrel and the cutting point in case the string should slip slightly in the barrel the first time you tune it up to concert pitch.

In the absence of wire cutters, a metal-based string end may be repeatedly bent back and forth until metal fatigue causes it to snap.

Many guitarists prefer to coil unsightly string ends rather than cut or break them off. Personally I feel this is more trouble than it's worth, but just in case you want to have a go, here's how it should be done.

As with cutting, it is advisable to kink a wound string first.

A coin is then held against the string, at a point just beyond the kink.

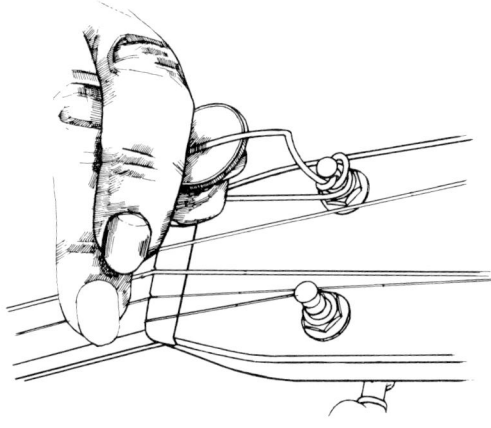

Then, with the edge of the coin pressing hard against the string, the hand is rapidly pulled away.

This causes the free end to coil like a spring,

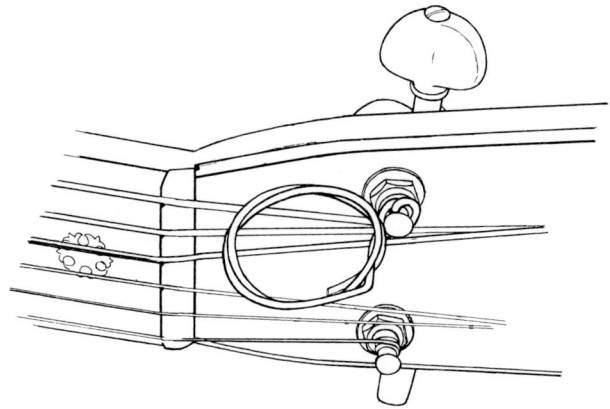

and allows it to be rolled tidily.

TUNING YOUR GUITAR

The standard tuning for the guitar is:

E A D G B E

. . . and there are several ways to get your guitar in tune.

USING A SET OF PITCH PIPES

These are six little reed pipes which look rather like a miniature pipes of Pan and sound very much like a mouth organ.

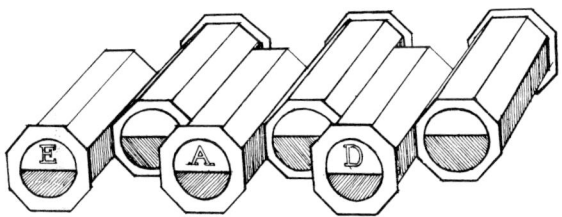

There is one pipe for each string of the guitar, so all you have to do is blow each pipe in turn — and tune the corresponding string.

There are three major drawbacks, however, to this method of getting your guitar in tune. Firstly, all pitch pipes have a tendency to "overblow" if too much air is blown through them. This produces a false pitch, somewhat sharper (higher) than the natural note of the pipe. Secondly, the notes produced by a set of pitch pipes are an octave *above* the pitch of a guitar.

In other words, each string of your guitar must be tuned eight notes lower than the note blown on the pipe.

This really isn't too much of a disadvantage as long as you are aware of the pitch difference. Most people compensate quite automatically for octaves. For instance, if a man is asked to duplicate a note sung by a woman soprano, he will, without really thinking about it, sing it an octave lower.

A far greater disadvantage is that very many people seem to have difficulty in matching a note produced by a blown reed with one sounded by a plucked string. For these people to use pitch pipes, tuning up quickly becomes agony. No matter how close they tune, the guitar and pipe always sound out of tune with each other.

Pitch pipes, however, are very inexpensive and would probably be a useful buy as long as you don't depend on them to give you perfect accuracy, but rather use them as a guide for NOTING.

TUNING BY NOTING

This is a much more accurate way to tune up your guitar.

Firstly we have to tune the sixth string to its correct note.

Do you remember what that is?

That's right, E.

You can use a piano or a pitch pipe or even a tuning fork.

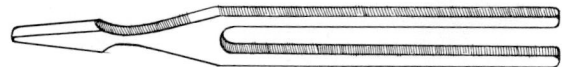

Have you done that?

Right! Now, we know that the strings of the guitar should be tuned E A D G B E, and we have the sixth string (E) already in tune. How do we tune the others?

Well, you may remember that when I was talking about how a guitar worked, I mentioned the FRET BARS, which are inlaid along the fingerboard. I told you then that they were used to shorten the vibrating length of a string—and, by doing so, raise its pitch.

Now, each fret bar or fret raises the pitch of a string by *half* a tone, which is called a HALFTONE or SEMITONE.

So if you hold a string down behind the first fret and then pluck it, the sound produced is one halftone *higher* than the normal note of the string.

If you hold the string down behind the second fret and pluck it, then the sound is *two* halftones higher, or one whole tone.

Three frets, and the sound is three halftones up from the normal note. In other words, one and a half tones higher.

Right! Now, we have our sixth string already tuned to E, and we must now find a way of tuning up the other five strings, A D G B and high E.

This is the way we are going to do it.

Take a careful look at this halftone diagram.

A	Bb	B	C	C#	D	Eb	E	F	F#	G	Ab and back to A

You'll see that A—the fifth-string note—is five halftones up from E.

Now, we already have the sixth string tuned to E—so we can use this string to help us tune the fifth.

It's easy. Look!

Each fret on the guitar raises the pitch of a string by one halftone,

so when the sixth string, E, is held down behind the fifth fret and plucked, it will give us the note of A—the note to which we must tune the fifth string.

Try it.

When you hold down the sixth string behind the fifth fret, it gives us the note of A.

OK?

So, turn the fifth string tuning button and raise the pitch of the string until it sounds the same as the fretted sixth string.

When the two notes match, your fifth string is in tune.

Right! You've got E and A. The next string must be tuned to D.

Look at the diagram once more.

A	B♭	B	C	C♯	D	E♭	E	F	F♯	G	A♭

How many steps are there between A and D?

That's right, five.

Count them: B flat (B♭), B, C, C Sharp (C♯) and D.

So if the fifth string, A, is held down behind the fifth fret, it will give us the note of D—the note to which we must tune the fourth string.

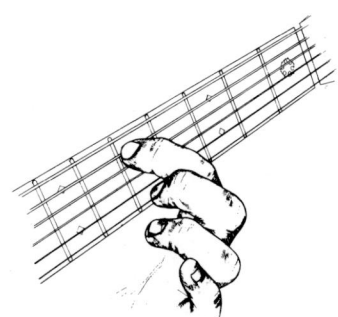

As before, adjust the pitch until the two notes sound the same.

OK?

Right! The next string, the third, must be tuned to G.

Once more, take a glance at the diagram.

A	B♭	B	C	C♯	D	E♭	E	F	F♯	G	A♭

That's right. It's another gap of five halftones, so hold your fourth string down behind the fifth fret, pluck it . . .

and tune your third string up to this note. The note of G.

Not so difficult, is it?

Now for the second string, which must be tuned to the note of B.

How many steps between the notes of G and B?

A	B♭	B	C	C♯	D	E♭	E	F	F♯	G	A♭

Four. A♭, A, B♭ and B.

Holding your third string, G, down behind the fourth fret, pluck it,

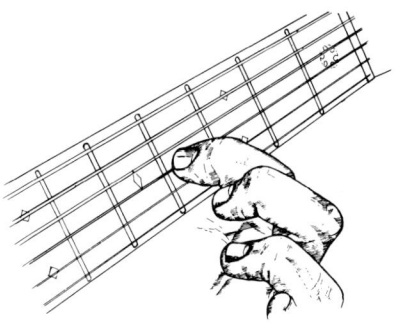

and tune your second string up to this new note—the note of B.

Just one more string to go; the first string, high E.

How many steps between B and E?

A	B♭	B	C	C♯	D	E♭	E	F	F♯	G	A♭

C, C♯, D, E♭ and E—five.

To tune the last string, E, just hold down the second string, B, behind the fifth fret,

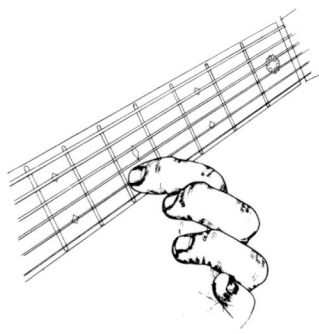

and you know the rest!

So your guitar is now in tune: E A D G B E.

The first string, E, is two octaves above the E on the sixth string. Can you hear it?

OK. Now, the next thing to do is to go back across the strings and check that they haven't slipped out of tune. Particularly with nylon-based strings, you'll find that it may take a day or two before a new set of strings stretches out and holds its pitch. So, before we go any further, starting with the low E string, check 'em again.

HOLDING THE GUITAR

The most important thing to consider when you're holding the
guitar is your comfort. If you don't feel comfortable, or at ease, then
your music will not sound relaxed either. This doesn't mean that
you should let yourself slouch and become sloppy, unless that's the
kind of music you want to play. You can, of course, get a strap and
play with the guitar around your neck, but while you're learning,
I'd advise you to spend the strap money on a better—or a new—
set of strings and play sitting down—like this:

Or like this:

Notice that in both positions the back is straight. Now, many guitarists and most classical players also use a footstool. I usually lose mine about three days out on a concert tour, so I've developed a way of resting one foot upon the other, that serves me fine. If you find this awkward, you could always rest your foot on your closed guitar case (you *do* have a case, don't you?).

Now, the same freedom of choice also extends to your right-hand position—with a few important provisos, however.

Look at this, a good position:

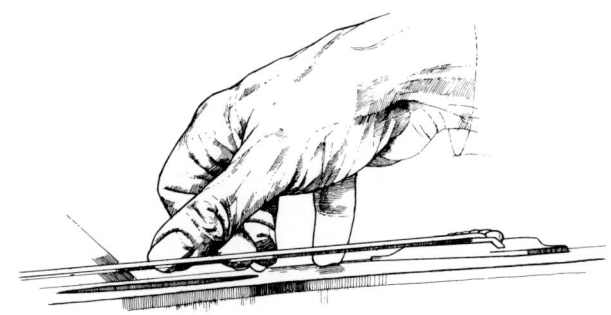

Notice that the thumb should always be in advance of the fingers. The hand attitude here:

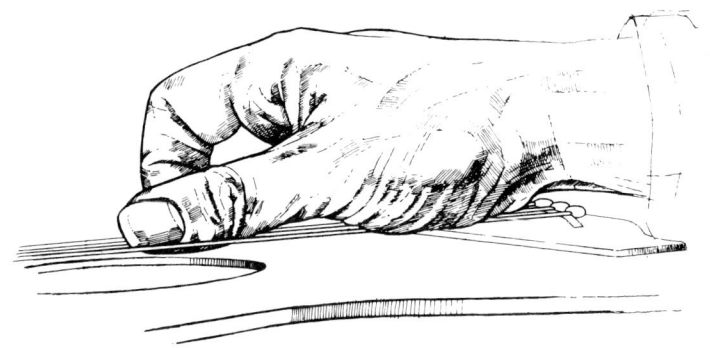

is very cramping and should be avoided. However, the use of the little finger to brace the hand on the table—while frowned upon by classical musicians—is widely used and quite acceptable.

NAILS

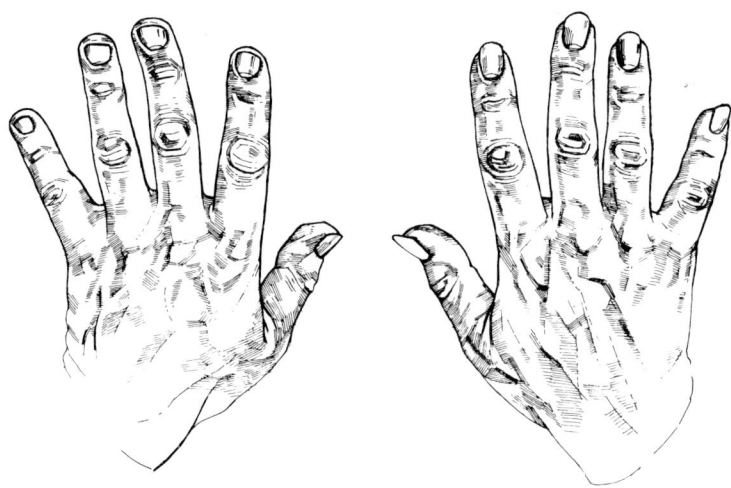

The nails on your left hand should be kept as short as possible, in order to allow the fingertips to stand vertically on the fingerboard when FRETTING, or pushing down a string. If the nails are too long, the finger will lean over at a slight angle, allowing the fleshy pad of the fingertip to lie against the neighboring string, and so deaden it. The nails of the right hand, however, should be allowed to grow a short way past the end of the fingertips. If your nails are brittle or too soft, or if you want to make a great deal of noise, you can buy a THUMBPICK and a set of FINGERPICKS from your local music shop,

or you can strengthen your nails so that they won't break. A method which I use is to soak small pieces of fine tissue paper in clear nail polish (lacquer), and then place them on the nail, smoothing away excess polish with a finger dipped in nail polish remover, and placing piece upon piece until a really thick lamination has been built up. After you've stuck about five or six pieces on each nail, let them dry and harden for a few hours, and then finish off by sealing each nail with a couple of coats of clear polish. Every week or so, when the polish starts to discolor, you can strip off the laminations by rubbing each nail firmly with a piece of cotton soaked in polish remover, refile them to the correct length, and slap on a new lamination. It'll save you lots of broken nails.

CHORD WINDOWS

Well, your guitar is tuned, hopefully, and you are sitting comfortably. Now is the time to start making some melodious sounds. Look at this diagram:

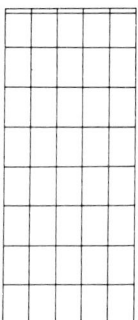

It's called a chord window, and it's a simplified picture of part of your guitar fingerboard.

The six vertical lines are the strings.

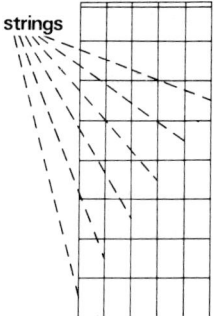

strings

first fret

second

third

fourth

fifth

sixth

seventh

The six horizontal lines are the frets.

And the heavy double line at the top is the bone top fret, or NUT.

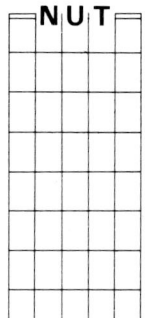

Guitarists use these windows to write down how they finger a chord. Look at this:

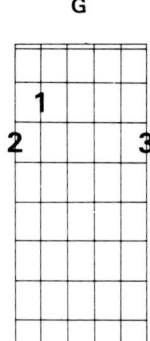

It's a window for the chord of G.

The tip of the first finger, left hand, is holding down the fifth string just behind the second fret.

The tip of the second finger, left hand, is holding down the sixth string just behind the third fret.

The tip of the third finger, left hand, is holding down the first string just behind the third fret.

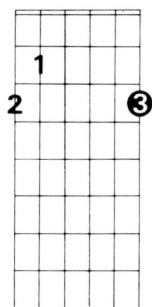

Now, still holding down the chord, strum gently across the strings with the thumb of your right hand.

How does it sound?

Are there any muffled strings?

Pluck the strings one at a time.

How does that sound?

If any strings sound dead or muffled it's probably due to one of three things:

    1. Maybe you're not holding down the chord firmly enough. Try bracing your thumb behind the guitar neck,

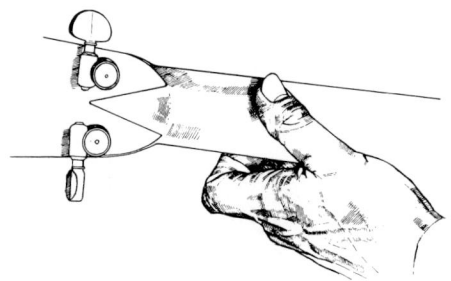

    and pushing with it. You'll find it makes chord holding much easier.

    2. Maybe your fingertips are not *just behind* the fret. If you put your fingertips too far behind the fret it's almost impossible to get a good sound.

3. Maybe one or more of your fingers are leaning over, causing the fleshy pad to deaden a neighboring string.

Check your fingering and try again.

Sounds better?

Good.

Here's another window for you.

It's the window for the chord of C.

The first finger is holding down (fretting) the second string just behind the first fret.

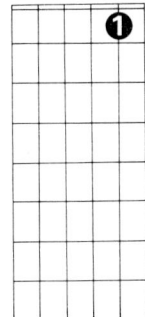

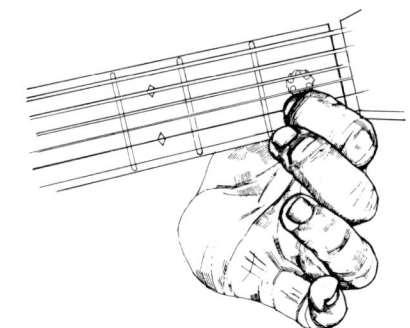

The second finger is fretting the fourth string just behind the second fret.

And the third finger is fretting the fifth string just behind the third fret.

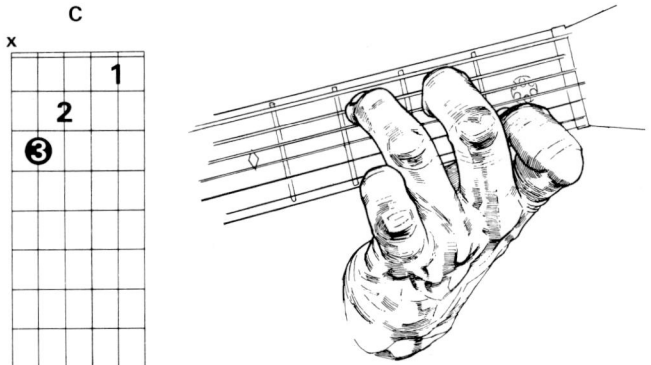

Try it.

How did you get on?

Did you notice a small X marked above the sixth string on your window? That X means that the sixth string is silent. In other words, in this chord we won't be playing on the sixth string.

So when you practice it, only pluck the fifth, fourth, third, second and first strings.

G

Right. Now play your G chord once more, strumming across the strings with your right-hand thumb.

Now your C chord. Remember not to play your sixth string.

C

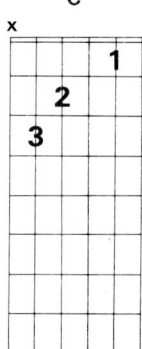

G

Now back to G.

C

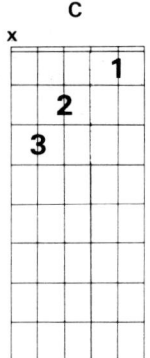

And C again:

Practice changing your left-hand fingering from G to C and back again. While your fingertips are cooling off, how about checking your tuning?

D7

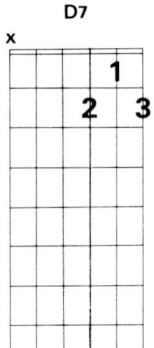

Right, here's another chord window for you: the chord of D7.

Your first finger frets the second string just behind the first fret.

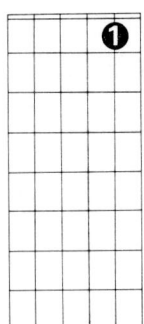

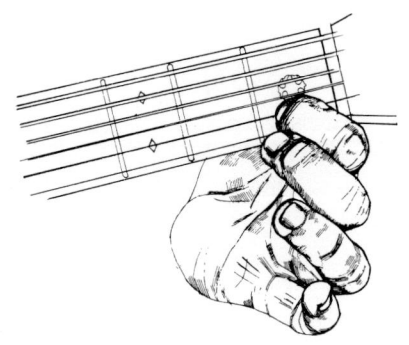

Your second finger frets the third string just behind the second fret.

Finally, the third finger frets the first string just behind the second fret.

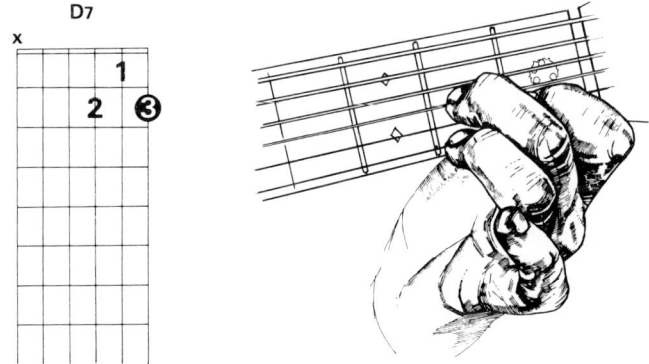

Again, the X over the sixth string warns us not to play it in this chord.

Try it.

How did you get on?

Remember the three-point checklist for muffled strings.

OK. Rest your hands for a moment.

For the first few days you'll find your fingertips will get very tender. But don't lose heart—they'll soon toughen up. Remember, every great guitar player was at the same stage as you at one time in his life.

Right, now I want you to play over your three chords in this order:

1   G (strum four times)   2   D7 (strum four times)

3   C (strum four times)   4   G (strum four times)

It sounds good, doesn't it? That's because G, C and D7 when played together make up a chord sequence—a chord sequence in the key of G major.

Try it again:

1   G (strum four times)   2   D7 (strum four times)

3   C (strum four times)   4   G (strum four times)

Rather like a circle, isn't it?

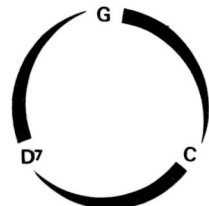

Right, let's give your left hand another rest for a minute or two and turn our attention to your right hand.

Place your third fingertip on the first string, your second fingertip on the second string, and your first fingertip on the third string.

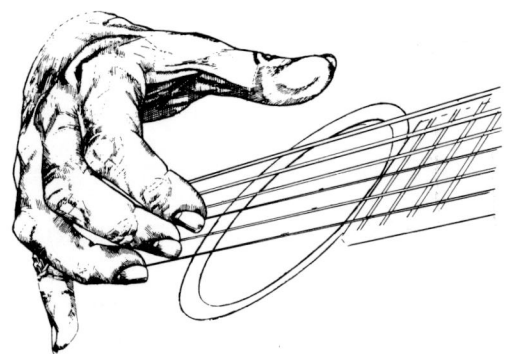

OK. Now, hold down your G chord with the left hand:

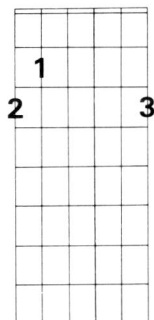

Pluck the sixth string with your right-hand thumb.

The sound is DUM.

Do it again. Hold down your G chord, and pluck the sixth string with your right-hand thumb.

DUM.

Good. Now, are your right-hand fingers still on the strings, or have they wandered off?   No matter, put them back.

Third finger on the first string, second finger on the second string, first finger on the third string.

Now, still holding your G chord with the left hand, pluck all three strings with all three fingers simultaneously.

The sound is CHING!

Try it again.

Third on first string, second on second string, and first on third string.

Together pluck—CHING!

Very good.

OK. Relax your hands for a moment, get up and walk about the room for a few minutes, make a cup of coffee, straighten out those cramped finger joints.

When you're ready, try again.

OK? Here we go then.

Hold down your G chord.

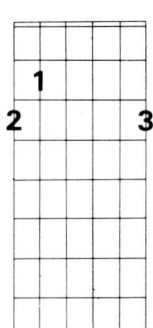

Rest your right-hand fingers so:
  —the first on the third string
  —second on the second string
  —third on the first string.

Right, now pluck the sixth string with your right hand thumb— DUM.

And then play your finger pluck on the three strings—CHING.

And again—DUM CHING.

And again—DUM CHING DUM CHING.

As you play the movements, count the rhythm out like this:

ONE TWO, ONE TWO, ONE TWO.

Good. Relax your hands again.

The next thing we're going to do is to try the new right-hand movement on our two other chords, C and D7.

Here they are again, together with the G chord:

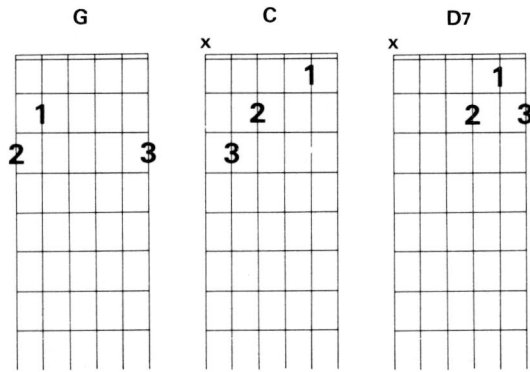

OK. Hold down the G chord once more, and off we go:

DUM CHING   DUM CHING   DUM CHING   DUM CHING

Now put your left-hand fingers in position for playing the chord of C, and play your right-hand movements again. This time, however, your thumb must pluck the fifth string (remember the X on the window).

DUM CHING   DUM CHING   DUM CHING   DUM CHING

OK. Now, change to the chord of D7. Still using the fifth string for your thumb, play your right-hand movement.

DUM CHING   DUM CHING   DUM CHING   DUM CHING

Finally, back to your old favorite, the chord of G, and the sixth-string thumb note:

DUM CHING   DUM CHING   DUM CHING   DUM CHING

How did you get on?

Try it over for yourself:

G	DUM CHING	DUM CHING	DUM CHING	DUM CHING
C	DUM CHING	DUM CHING	DUM CHING	DUM CHING
D7	DUM CHING	DUM CHING	DUM CHING	DUM CHING
G	DUM CHING	DUM CHING	DUM CHING	DUM CHING

The most important thing in guitar playing is good coordination. So as you practice, try to get both hands moving smoothly in their respective movements.

For instance, you should aim to change from one chord fingering to the next with ease and confidence. And to help you, you could try practicing in front of a mirror. Watching your reflected finger changes, you'll see any awkward movements much more clearly than you would craning down over the fingerboard.

Always use as little finger movement as possible when changing chords. If you flap your fingers around in between chords, you stand much more chance of ending up on the wrong strings. This economy of movement also applies to your right-hand style. If you lift your whole hand away on the finger-pluck stroke, you'll find it difficult to land your fingers on the correct strings again.

So, don't move your hand, just move your fingers,

OK?

Now, the rhythm of the right-hand stroke was:

ONE TWO   ONE TWO   ONE TWO

So we call it a DOUBLE-TIME style. This just means that it's a style for using if you have a tune with two beats to the bar—a TWO-FOUR tune.

The rhythm is rather like marching feet:

tramp	tramp	tramp	tramp	tramp	tramp
1	2	1	2	1	2

You can also use it for a QUADRUPLE-TIME tune. This just means a tune with four beats to the bar—a FOUR-FOUR tune.

The rhythm sounds like this:

tramp	tramp	tramp	tramp	tramp	tramp	tramp	tramp
1	2	3	4	1	2	3	4

Next is a tune in which you can try out your new chords and finger style.

"THREE BLIND MICE"

```
   G      D7    G
Three  blind  mice
  1 2    1 2   1 2     1 2


   G      D7    G
Three  blind  mice

  1 2    1 2    1 2    1 2
 G    C          G
See  how  they  run
1 2   1    2    1 2   1 2
 G    C          G
See  how  they  run
1 2   1    2    1 2    1

        G                  D7              G
They  ran  down  the  road  and  the  farmer's  wife
 2     1      2      1       2     1 2        1

        G              D7          G
She   cut   off  their  tails  with  a  carving  knife
 2     1      2     1      2    1 2     1

               D7           G
Did  you  ever  see  such  a  thing  in  your  life
   2      1 2   1      2    1    2      1

             D7   G
As  three  blind  mice?
 2   1 2   1 2     1
```

Right, now before you start, let's look it over and see if you understand how to play it.

Above the words of the song I've marked the chords that your left hand should be holding down:

G on THREE, D7 on BLIND and so on.

Don't let all those changes bother you. Your left hand is going to be busy, but you can play the tune as slowly as you like.

Now, beneath the words I've marked the right-hand style.

The "1" means your thumb pluck, and the "2" is the pluck with your fingers together.

Let's try the first line together.

Rest your right-hand fingers so:

    —the first on the third string

    —second on the second string

    —third on the first string.

Hold down a chord of G with your left hand.

G

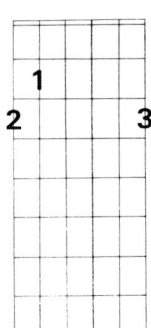

Here we go:

THREE	Pluck the sixth string with your thumb.	Count ONE
	Pluck the third, second and first strings simultaneously with the first, second and third fingers.	Count TWO

Hold down a chord of D7 with your left hand.

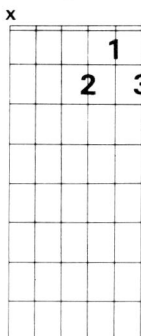

BLIND   Pluck the fifth string with your thumb.   Count ONE
(We don't play the sixth string in this
chord, remember?)

Pluck the third, second and first strings   Count TWO
simultaneously with the first, second and
third fingers.

Hold down a chord of G with your left hand.

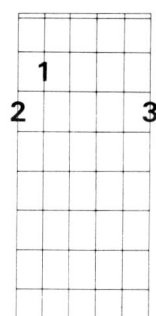

MICE   Pluck the sixth string with your thumb.   Count ONE

Pluck the third, second and first strings   Count TWO
simultaneously with the first, second
and third fingers.

Now to complete the line, we play our style once more, still holding down a chord of G.

This leads us to the second line, which is exactly the same as the one we've just played.

Try it.

How did you get on? Not so bad is it?

Let's look at the third line.

Watch out for HOW THEY.

You must play the thumb-pluck ONE on HOW.

And the finger-pluck TWO on THEY.

Not too awkward, though, is it?

Right! Try the line through on your own, then put it together with the first two lines.

Now, the fourth line is exactly the same as line three, except that the extra linking bar at the end carries over to the fifth line. Look:

```
     See   how   they   run
     1 2    1     2     1 2    1

     They   ran   down   the
      2      1      2
```

This just means that as you play the TWO part of your style in the link, you start singing THEY.

Try it.

Now let's turn our attention to the fifth line.

```
They   ran   down   the   road   and   the   farmer's   wife
 2      1      2      1     1      2     1      1 2       1
```

There are two instances of "linked words," but they shouldn't cause you any worry as they are just there to show you that both words should be sung on one beat.

The rest of the tune is very straightforward, so why not go back to the start and try it through to the end?

A TRIPLE-TIME STYLE AND A NEW KEY—D MAJOR

Here's a style that will enable you to play tunes which are written in TRIPLE, or WALTZ time.

Hold down a G chord.

Count ONE	Pluck the sixth string with your thumb.
Count TWO	Pluck the third, second and first strings with your first, second and third fingers.
Count THREE	Repeat as for count TWO.

The rhythm is:

ONE TWO THREE,   ONE TWO THREE,   ONE TWO THREE

DUM CHING CHING, DUM CHING CHING, DUM CHING CHING

It's just like your double-time style, but with part TWO repeated. Instead of:

ONE TWO,   ONE TWO,   ONE TWO,   ONE TWO,

it's: ONE TWO THREE,   ONE TWO THREE,   ONE TWO THREE

Right, here's a new key for you, the key of D MAJOR:

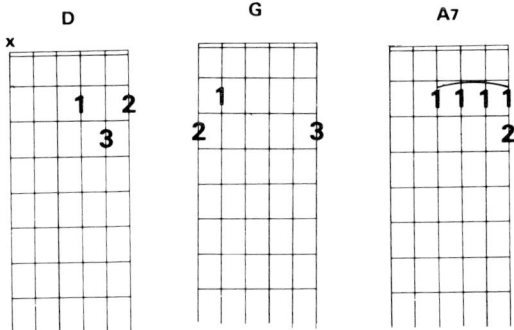

You already know how to play the second chord, don't you?

Here's the chord of D.

The tip of the first finger is fretting the third string just behind the second fret.

The tip of the second finger is fretting the first string just behind the second fret.

The tip of the third finger is fretting the second string just behind the third fret.   Try it.

Did you notice the X above the sixth string? That's right, we don't play it in this chord.

Don't forget to hold the strings down firmly, just behind the frets.

Now for the chord of A7. Here it is:

It's unlike the other chords I've shown you in that your first finger
has to lie like a short stick across the first four strings. We call this
a BARRE.

You may find it difficult at first to hold the strings down firmly
enough to stop them from buzzing, so here's a tip to help you:
whenever you hold down any chord fingering, you'll find that if you
brace your thumb more firmly against the guitar neck, your fingers
will exert more pressure on the strings which you are holding down.

Try it.

See what I mean?

OK. Let's play over your new chord sequence using the triple-time
style.

Under each first count I've marked a string which you should
pluck with your thumb. If you play the strings I've marked, you'll
find the alternating bass notes help to swing the style along.

As you play, count the beats aloud, accenting the first—the thumb
stroke—very slightly:

     ONE TWO THREE   **ONE** TWO THREE   **ONE** TWO THREE

Here's another song for you to learn.

"DOWN IN THE VALLEY"

D
Down in   the   val – ley
 1   2   3   1 2 3 1 2 3   12
(5)   (4)   (4)   (5)

                 A7
The   val – ley   so   low
 3   1   2   3   1 2 3   1 2 3   1 2 3
    (4)   (4)   (5)   (4)

Hang   your   head   o – ver
 1   2   3   1 2 3 1 2 3   1 2 3
(5)   (5)   (6)   (5)

              G   D
Hear   the   wind   blow
 1   2   3   1 2 3   1 2 3 1 2 3
(5)   (6)   (5)   (4)

Hear   the   wind   blow,   love
 1   2   3   1 2 3   1 2 3   1 2 3
(5)   (4)   (4)   (5)

              A7
Hear   the   wind   blow
 1   2   3   1 2 3 1 2 3 1 2 3
(4)   (4)   (5)   (4)

```
Hang   your   head   o – ver
 1       2      3     1 2 3   1 2 3   1 2 3
(5)                  (5)'    (6)    (5)
```

```
                      D     G     D
Hear   the   wind   blow
 1      2     3      1 2 3   1 2 3   1 2 3   1
(5)                 (4)            (4)    (4)
```

Down in the valley
The valley so low
Hang your head o – ver
Hear the wind blow

    Hear the wind blow, love
    Hear the wind blow
    Hang your head o – ver
    Hear the wind blow

Going to build me a castle
Forty feet high
Just so I can see you
As you're riding by

Now, roses love sunshine
And violets love dew
And the angels in Heaven
They know I love you

So, if you don't love me
Go and love whom you please
But put your arms round me
And give my heart ease

Down in the valley
The valley so low
Hang your head o – ver
Hear the wind blow

As before, I've marked the rhythm out for you beneath the words, and I've also suggested some attractive bass notes for your thumb to pluck on the first counts. This doesn't mean that you shouldn't experiment for yourself. It would probably help you if you sang the counts through first without the guitar.

Rest your right hand on your right knee and as you sing the counts try to follow them with your right-hand finger and thumb movements.

Don't take the song too fast, but see if you can keep up a relaxed, swinging tempo.

When you can count it through, miming the finger and thumb movements, try singing through the words, again going through the hand movements on your knee.

How did you get on?

Now, if you can sing it through with the hand movements, try the song through with your guitar. You'll find that it almost plays itself.

Here's another three-four style for you to learn:

Hold down a chord of D.

Count ONE	Thumb plucks a bass string, say the fourth.
Count TWO	Index finger plucks the third string.
Count THREE	Middle and ring fingers pluck the second and first strings together.

The sound is: DUM ER CHING

Try it, emphasizing the first count:

ONE TWO THREE   **ONE** TWO THREE   **ONE** TWO THREE

How about trying it out on "Down in the Valley"?

A SIX-EIGHT STYLE

If you double up a triple-time you get a SEXTUPLE or SIX-EIGHT tempo.

One of the most effective six-eight accompanying styles is achieved by extending the last style like this:

Hold down a chord of D.

Count ONE	Thumb plucks a bass string, say the fourth.
Count TWO	Index finger plucks the third string.
Count THREE	Middle and ring fingers pluck the second and first strings.
Count FOUR	Index finger plucks the third string.
Count FIVE	Middle and ring fingers pluck the second and first strings.
Count SIX	Index finger plucks the third string.

The sound is: DUM ER CHING ER CHING ER

Here is "Down in the Valley" again, but this time written out so that you can practice your six-eight style.

Again, should you have any difficulty getting the counts to fall in the right places, lay your guitar down and count the song out on your knee.

DOWN IN THE VALLEY

```
 D
Down   in    the   val – ley
 1 2   3 4   5 6   1 2 3 4 5 6   1 2 3 4 5 6   1 2 3 4
(5)                (4)           (4)           (5)


                    A7
The   val – ley   so   low
5 6   1 2 3 4   5 6   1 2 3 4 5 6   1 2 3 4 5 6   1 2 3 4 5 6
      (4)            (4)           (5)           (4)


Hang   your   head   o – ver
 1 2   3 4   5 6   1 2 3 4 5 6   1 2 3 4 5 6   1 2 3 4 5 6
(5)                (5)           (6)           (5)


                    G                         D
Hear   the   wind   blow
 1 2   3 4   5 6   1 2 3 4 5 6   1 2 3 4 5 6   1 2 3 4 5 6
(5)                (6)           (5)           (4)


Hear   the   wind   blow,   love
 1 2   3 4 — 5 6   1 2 3 4 5 6   1 2 3 4 5 6   1 2 3 4 5 6
(5)                (4)           (4)           (5)


                    A7
Hear   the   wind   blow
 1 2   34    5 6   1 2 3 4 5 6   1 2 3 4 5 6   1 2 3 4 5 6
(4)                (4)           (5)           (4)


Hang   your   head   o   ver
 1 2   3 4   5 6   1 2 3 4 5 6   1 2 3 4 5 6   1 2 3 4 5 6
(5)                (5)           (6)           (5)


                    D           G           D
Hear   the   wind   blow
 1 2   3 4   5 6   1 2 3 4 5 6   1 2 3 4 5 6   1 2 3 4 5 6   1
(5)                (4)           (6)           (4)           (4)
```

All right-hand styles for the guitar fall into one of two categories: they're either PLUCKING styles (PICKS) or STRUMMING styles (SCRATCHES).

The styles that I've been showing you so far are picking styles.

Here they are again:

STYLE 1

Two-Four Pick

Count ONE	Thumb plucks a bass string.
Count TWO	Index, middle and ring fingers pluck the third, second and first strings together.

The sound is: DUM CHING

STYLE 2

Three-Four Pick

Count ONE	Thumb plucks a bass string.
Count TWO	Index, middle and ring fingers pluck the third, second and first strings together.
Count THREE	Index, middle and ring fingers pluck the third, second and first strings together.

The sound is: DUM CHING CHING

STYLE 3

Three-Four Pick Variation

Count ONE	Thumb plucks a bass string.
Count TWO	Index finger plucks the third string.
Count THREE	Middle and ring fingers pluck the second and first strings together.

The sound is: DUM ER CHING

STYLE 4

Six-Eight Pick

Count ONE	Thumb plucks a bass string.
Count TWO	Index finger plucks the third string.
Count THREE	Middle and ring fingers pluck the second and first strings.
Count FOUR	Index finger plucks the third string.
Count FIVE	Middle and ring fingers pluck the second and first strings.
Count SIX	Index finger plucks the third string.

The sound is: DUM ER CHING ER CHING ER

Before we leave the basic picking styles, here is a QUADRUPLE-TIME (four-four) pick, which is not only marvelous on its own, but alternated with the two-four pick makes a very professional-sounding accompaniment.

STYLE 5

Four-Four Pick

Count ONE	Thumb plucks a bass string.
Count TWO	Index finger plucks the third string.
Count THREE	Middle and ring fingers pluck the second and first strings.
Count FOUR	Index finger plucks the third string.

The sound is: DUM ER CHING ER

Practice it until it sounds confident, then experiment with mixing the two-four and four-four picks.

Here's one combination that I use very often.

1	2	1	2	1	2	3	4	1	2
2/4		2/4		4/4				2/4	

Another good mixture is:

1	2	1	2	3	4	1	2	3	4	1	2
2/4			4/4				4/4			2/4	

See what you can figure out for yourself.

How did you get on?

You can also get attractive accompaniments by combining three-four and six-eight picks, but I'll leave you to experiment.

The next styles that we come to all fall into the category of scratches.

Before you start on them, however, it would be a good idea if you went back to the start and reviewed all that I've given you so far.

SCRATCH STYLES

Here we go with the first of our scratches.

THE DOUBLE-TIME (TWO-FOUR) SCRATCH

Hold down a chord of G.

Count ONE	Thumb plucks a bass string, say the sixth.
Count TWO	The back of the index fingernail grazes down across the remaining strings.

The sound is: DUM CHING

To get the best effect from this lick, you should try to give a good definite graze on the fingernail downstroke, count TWO. The best way to achieve this is to curl your finger up into your palm as you play count ONE with your thumb.

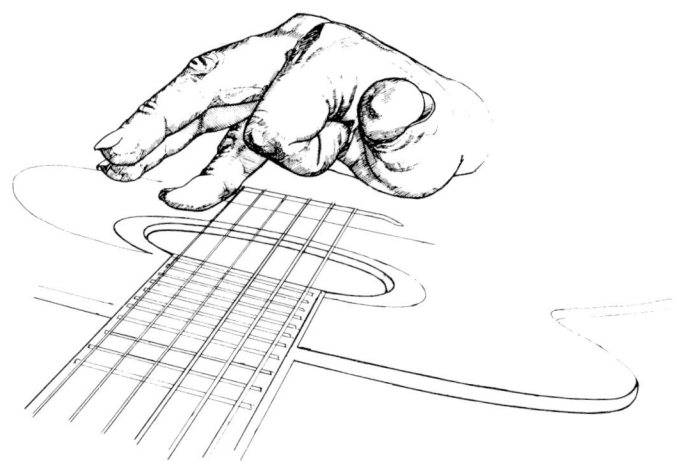

Then uncurl it, flicking it straight across the strings, for count TWO.

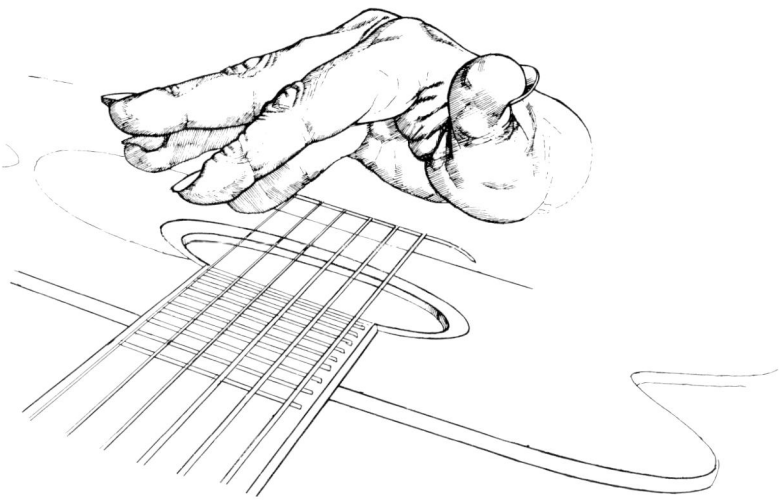

Try it.

How was it?

It's slightly harder than it appears, isn't it. Don't worry, you'll soon get the hang of it.

Remember what I told you,when I was showing you chord sequences about moving your hands as little as possible. This is doubly important when one is learning strumming techniques, as there is always a temptation to move the whole hand rather than just the thumb or fingers.

As you practice, count out the beats and try to get the style to skip along.

It should be light and bouncy, so look out for any tendency for it to sound wooden.

Play it through with your chord sequences, alternating the bass strings.

Then try it on your two-four song.

OK. Next is a very useful four-four scratch style.

FOUR-FOUR SCRATCH

Hold down a G chord again.

Count ONE	Thumb plucks a bass string, again we'll take the sixth.
Count TWO	Index fingernail grazes *up* across all the remaining strings.
Count THREE	Index fingernail grazes *down* across all the remaining strings.
Count FOUR	Index fingernail grazes *up* across all the remaining strings.

The sound is: DUM· ER CHING ER

This is a much more flowing style, so there is no need to play the finger down-grazes as forcefully as you did in the two-four scratch.

Of course, you can emphasize them if you like the effect that it gives—a typical "cowboy" lope—but it's not necessary.

As for the plucking styles, you can combine two-four and four-four scratch styles, too. Don't do it just yet, however. Wait till you're certain you can play them apart correctly. When you can, then experiment all you like.

Here's a song that you're sure to know, in which I've included both two-four and four-four scratches.

"JOHN BROWN'S BODY"

```
D
John   Brown's   body    lies    a – mould'ring   in    his   grave
1        2         1       2            1      2     3     4    1    2
      2/4               2/4                          4/4            2/4
  G
John   Brown's   body    lies    a – mould'ring   in    his  grave
1        2         1       2            1      2     3     4    1    2
      2/4               2/4                          4/4           2/4
D
John      Brown's     body     lies    a – mould'ring     in      his
1      2     3     4    1        2             1           2
         4/4                2/4                      2/4


                       A7                              D
grave     But     his    soul    goes    marching    on
  1        2              1    2    3    4   1   2   3   4   1   2   1   2
     2/4                      4/4             4/4           2/4     2/4
  D
Glory      glory     Hale  –  lu  –  jah
1 2 3 4     1 2        3 4      1 2 3 4    1 2 3 4
4/4              4/4           4/4         4/4
  G                         D
Glory      glory     Hale  –  lu  –  jah
1 2          1          2       1 2       1 2
2/4              2/4           2/4       2/4

Glory      glory     Hale  –  lu  –  jah
1 2 3 4     1 2        3 4      1 2 3 4    1
4/4              4/4           4/4         2/4

                    A7                            D
But      his    soul    goes    marching    on
2              1      2     1   2    1   2          1
                  2/4           2/4        2/4            2/4
```

TRIPLE-TIME (THREE-FOUR) SCRATCH

Let's move on to a triple-time scratch, which can also be doubled up to make a sextuple-time accompaniment.

Hold down a chord, say D.

Count ONE	Thumb plucks a bass string, say the fourth.
Count TWO	Index finger grazes *up* across the remaining strings.
Count THREE	Index finger grazes *down* across the remaining strings.

The sound is: DUM CHING CHING

You should accent the first count slightly:

ONE TWO THREE   **ONE** TWO THREE

Right! Now to turn it into a six-eight accompaniment, all you have to do is double it up:

Count ONE	Thumb plucks a bass string.
Count TWO	Index finger grazes *up* across the remaining strings.
Count THREE	Index finger grazes *down* across the remaining strings.
Count FOUR	Thumb plucks a bass string.
Count FIVE	Index finger grazes *up* across the remaining strings.
Count SIX	Index finger grazes *down* across the remaining strings.

And you should accent it so:

      ONE TWO THREE **FOUR** FIVE SIX

      ONE TWO THREE **FOUR** FIVE SIX

Simple, isn't it?

Before we go any further, you should now spend some time going back over what we've been learning so far. In particular, make sure that you know the chords and can change between them smoothly. To help you, it's a good idea to write out the chord names on a piece of paper, and have a friend call them out at random for you to play.

By the way, can you still remember how to tune your guitar? Why not slacken the strings off and see if you can get back in tune again without using the book.

LEARNING TABLATURE

Tablature is one of the oldest methods of writing down music for stringed instruments. Originally used by lutenists, it is generally accepted that the great Spanish musicologist Juan Carlos y Amat was the first to apply this simply understood music system to the guitar. The modern tablature system is even easier to learn than Amat's, consisting of a staff of six lines:

Each line represents one string of your guitar: the top line is the first string, the next the second, and so on down to the bottom-most line which represents the sixth string:

Numbers are marked on these lines:

And these tell us behind which fret a string should be held down in order to produce a note that we need.

For example, this tablature tells us that the sixth string is to be held down behind the third fret.

Now, if we need to play a string open—in other words, a string that isn't being held down by a finger—then that is shown by a zero.

In the example above, the first string must be played open (unfretted).

So, to recap, any string to be played is marked either:

1. By a number, to show behind which fret it must be held down, or

2. By a zero, if the string is to be played open.

If a string is not marked, you do *not* play it.

Now, above the staff are marked any chords which you'll need in order to play the tune.

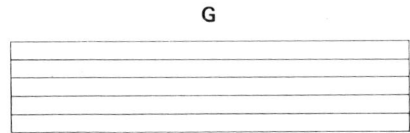

While below the staff are marked the fingers of the right hand which are to be used.

T = thumb   I = index finger   M = middle finger   R = ring finger

Look at this:

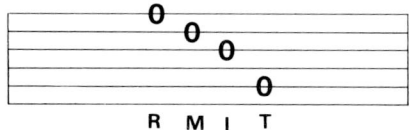

Can you see what you'd have to do in order to play it? That's right, your ring finger plucks the open first string, then your middle finger plucks the open second string, and this is followed by the index finger plucking the open third string. Finally, your thumb plucks the open fifth string.

Try it.

How about this then:

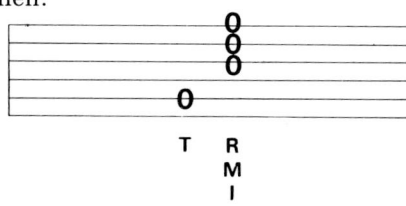

That's right, it's our basic two-four pluck style.

Count ONE Thumb plucks the open fifth string.

Count TWO Index finger plucks the open third string, middle finger plucks the open second string, and ring finger plucks the open first string, all together.

The sound is: DUM CHING

Look at this tablature:

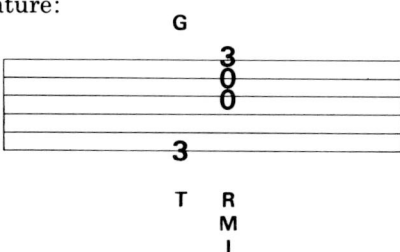

This time a chord is marked above the staff. If you hold down the chord, the chord of G, and then play the tablature, you'll find that both the first and sixth string are automatically held down behind the third fret.

Try it.

See what I mean? Both the first and sixth string are held down behind the third fret. Of course, in a G chord the fifth string is also fretted, behind the second fret.

So, we hold it down too, but because it's not marked on our tablature staff,

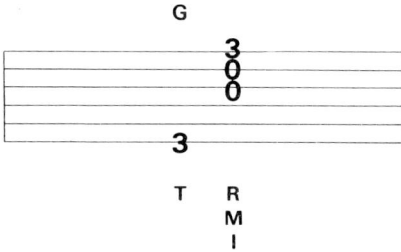

we don't actually play it.

Now, the style is in two-four time, isn't it? That means that there are two beats to the bar, like this:

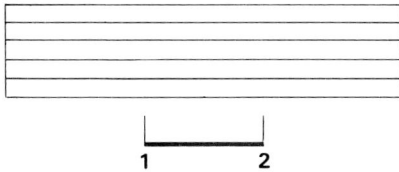

To show where the bar starts and finishes we have BAR LINES.

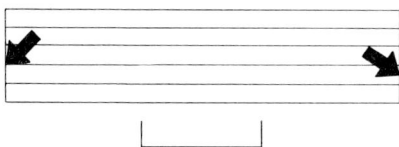

Here's the two-four pluck again, fully written out.

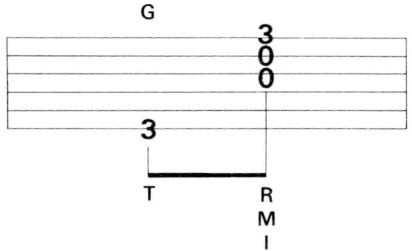

Isn't it easy to understand?

This is how the three-four pluck looks written down:

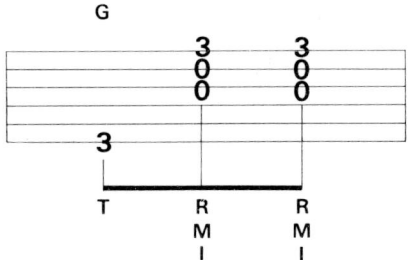

and the three-four pluck variation:

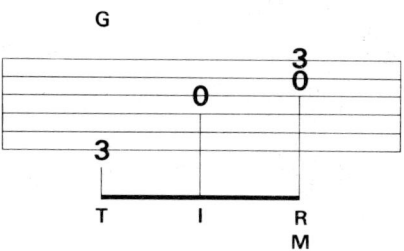

Now, look at this:

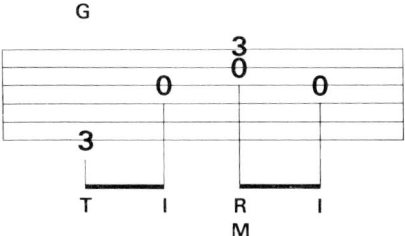

Yes, it's the four-four pluck.

When we write a four-four bar, we can either divide it or link all the notes like this:

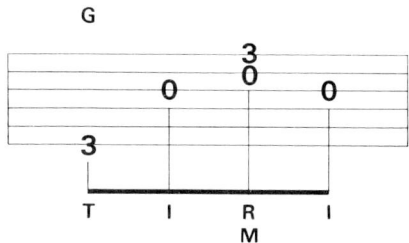

Either way is correct.

Similarly, we can write a six-eight bar either like this:

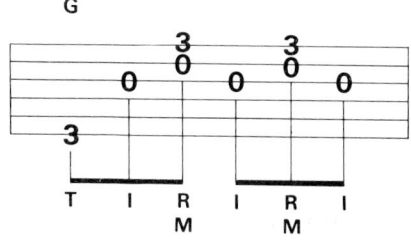

or like this:

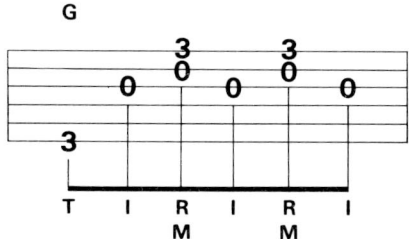

I tend to prefer divided bars as I think it makes them easier to read.

Let's have a look at some other signs that we use in tablature writing:

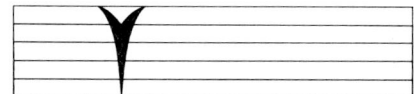

This is how we write a downward brush stroke, or scratch, across the strings, and here it is being used to illustrate the two-four scratch:

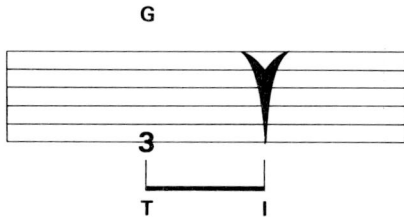

If you see the brush written like this:

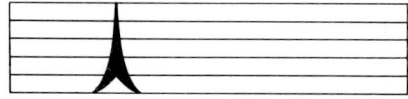

It means that the scratch or brush is upward.

The four-four scratch style therefore would look like this:

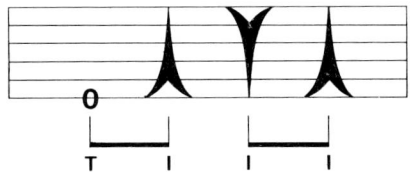

I think it's time I showed you how to play a melody using tablature; but before I do, go back over this explanation and make certain that you understand it.

PLAYING A MELODY

"When I First Came to This Land"

The easiest way to start melody playing is to use the bass strings.
Take a look at this:

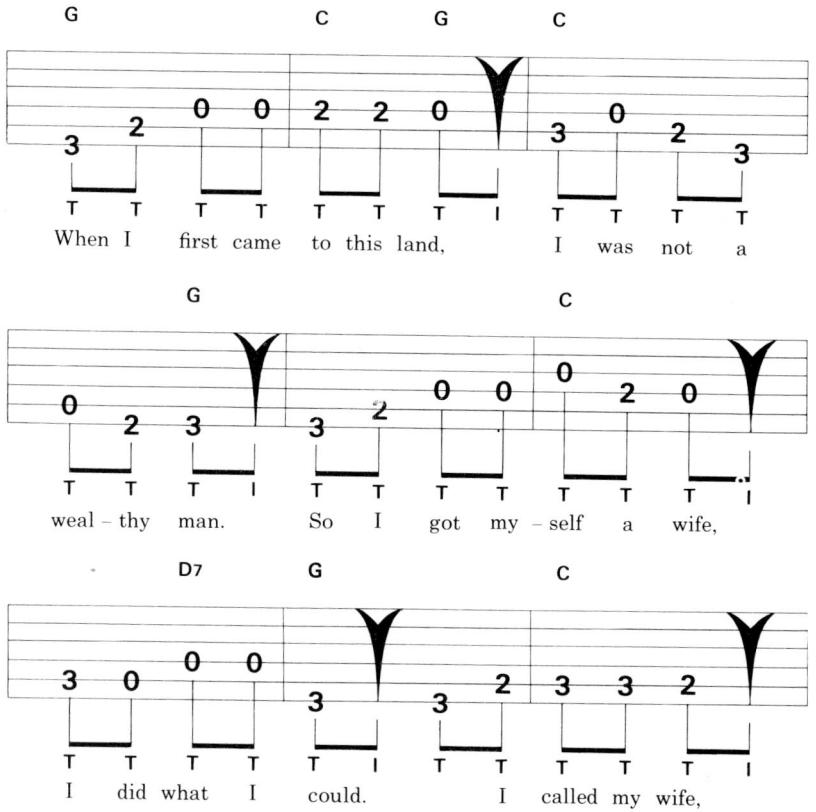

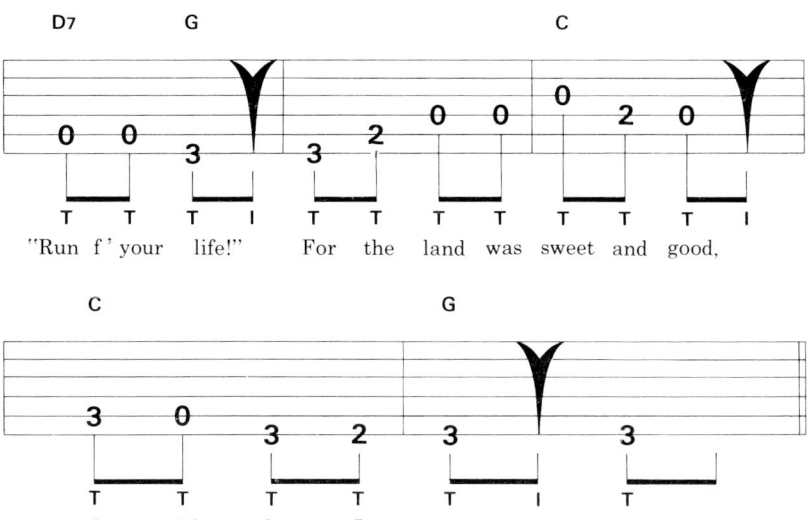

```
D7        G                              C
   0   0                    0   0   0    2   0
         3         3    2
   T   T    T   I   T   T   T   T   T   T   T   I
```
"Run f' your life!"   For the land was sweet and good,

```
C                       G
   3   0                    
         3    2    3         3
   T   T   T   T   T   I   T
```
I   did what I   could.

When I first came to this land
I was not a wealthy man.
So I got myself a wife,
I did what I could.
  I called my wife, "Run f' your life!"
  For the land was sweet and good,
  I did what I could.

When I first came to this land
I was not a wealthy man.
So I got myself a cow,
I did what I could.
  I called my cow, "No milk now!"
  I called my wife, "Run for your life!"
  For the land was sweet and good,
  I did what I could.

(The song continues with each chorus building upon all those which have gone before.)

. . . So I got myself a horse   I called my horse, "Fell off, of course!"

. . . So I got myself a donkey   I called my donkey, "Legs all wonkey!"

. . . So I got myself a plough   I called my plough, "Don't know how!"

. . . So I got myself a duck   I called my duck, "Such hard luck!"

. . . So I got myself a son   I called my son, "My work's done!"

Can you work out what the tempo is? That's right, it's four-four, because each bar contains four beats. Therefore the rhythm must be:

ONE TWO THREE FOUR   ONE TWO THREE FOUR

OK?

Here's how you play it.

BAR ONE

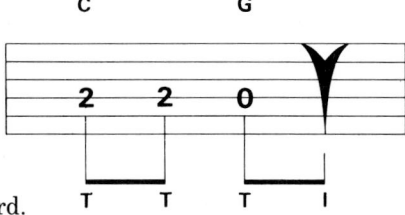

Hold down a G chord.

Count ONE	Thumb plucks the sixth string, held down behind the third fret.
Count TWO	Thumb plucks the fifth string, held down behind the second fret.
Count THREE	Thumb plucks the fourth string open.
Count FOUR	Thumb plucks the fourth string open.

BAR TWO

Change to C chord.

Count ONE	Thumb plucks the fourth string, held down behind the second fret.
Count TWO	Thumb plucks the fourth string, held down behind the second fret.

Change to G chord.

Count THREE	Thumb plucks the fourth string open.
Count FOUR	First finger grazes down across the remaining strings.

Right, now before we go any further, go back to the start and practice the first two bars. As you play them, count out the rhythm, and make certain that it doesn't vary. You should keep a steady
ONE TWO THREE FOUR   ONE TWO . . .

Don't let it become irregular, or the song will sound very ragged.

OK?

Let's play BAR THREE.

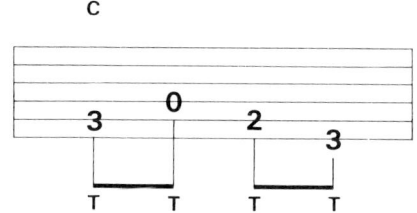

Hold down a C chord.

Count ONE	Thumb plucks the fifth string, held down behind the third fret.
Count TWO	Thumb plucks the fourth string open (in a chord of C this string would normally be held down behind the second fret by the left hand second finger; to play the string open, simply lift off the second finger and pluck it). OK?
Count THREE	Thumb plucks the fifth string, held down behind the second fret (the easiest finger to hold it down with is the second).
Count FOUR	Thumb plucks the sixth string, held down behind the third fret (easiest finger is the third).

BAR FOUR

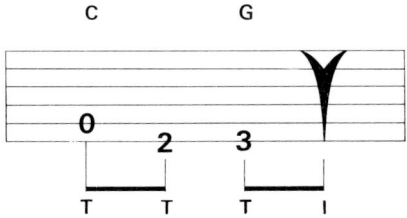

Count ONE   Thumb plucks the fifth string open (remove the fretting finger)

Count TWO   Thumb plucks the sixth string held down behind second fret (use your second finger).

Change to a chord of G.

Count THREE   Thumb plucks the sixth string held down behind the third fret.

Count FOUR   First finger grazes down across the remaining strings.

How are you getting along?

Now, go back to the start of the song and try singing the words as you're playing the melody.

Not too hard, is it?

Right, now if you look at BAR FIVE,

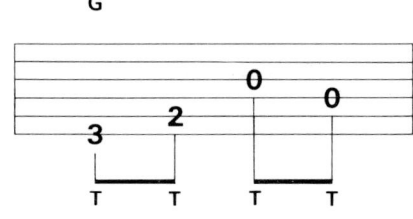

you'll see that it's exactly the same as BAR ONE,

while BAR SIX

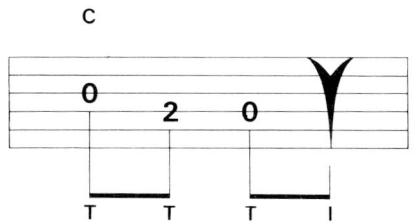

apart from the note on the first count, is the same as BAR TWO.
Let's move on then, to BAR SEVEN:

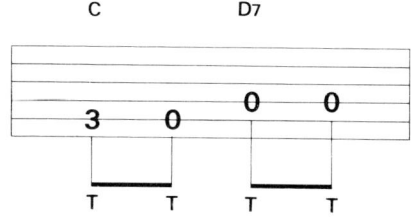

Hold down a chord of C.

      Count ONE   Thumb plucks the fifth string held down
                                behind the third fret.

      Count TWO   Thumb plucks the fifth string open.

Change to a chord of D7.

      Count THREE   Thumb plucks the fourth string open.

      Count FOUR   Thumb plucks the fourth string open.

Nothing difficult there then.

How about BAR EIGHT?

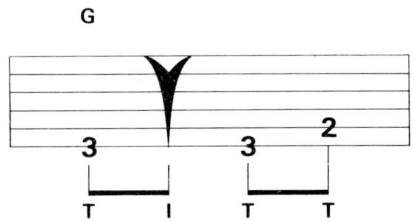

Hold down a chord of G.

Count ONE	Thumb plucks the sixth string held down behind the third fret.
Count TWO	Index finger grazes down across the remaining strings.
Count THREE	Thumb plucks the sixth string held down behind the third fret.
Count FOUR	Thumb plucks the fifth string held down behind the second fret.

And so on through the tune.

I really don't think that you need me to explain the remaining bars. You shouldn't find anything that you can't cope with. But if you do get stuck, just sit and think about it for a moment or two and you'll find the problem will solve itself . . . promise!

THE ROCKING BASS

I think it was Segovia who said that the guitar was an orchestra. By this he meant that not only can the player modulate the tone of the guitar to give the illusion of different instruments, but also that he can play both a melody and a simultaneous accompaniment.

In "When I First Came to This Land," we played a simple bass-line melody. Now we shall be playing melodies on the treble strings, *and* playing an accompaniment on the basses.

One way to do this is to use a ROCKING BASS.

Take up your guitar, but don't worry about holding a chord down. We'll be playing the strings open.

Count ONE	Thumb plucks the open sixth string.
Count TWO	Thumb plucks the open third string.
Count THREE	Thumb plucks the open sixth string.
Count FOUR	Thumb plucks the open third string.

The sound is: DUM TY DUM TY

Try it. Your thumb should rock between the strings with no hesitation.

Practice getting the swing really smooth and rhythmic. As you rock, count out the beats aloud:

ONE TWO THREE FOUR ONE TWO THREE FOUR

Don't pause at the end of a bar like this:

ONE TWO THREE FOUR   ONE TWO THREE FOUR

Join one rock to the next and try to get the thumb swing automatic. When your foot starts to tap, you're doing it right!

OK, now this is how it looks written down:

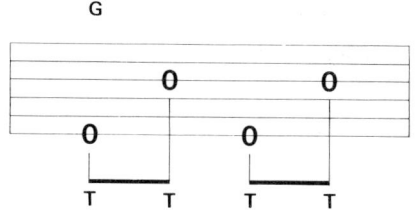

And here's how it looks if you hold down a chord of G:

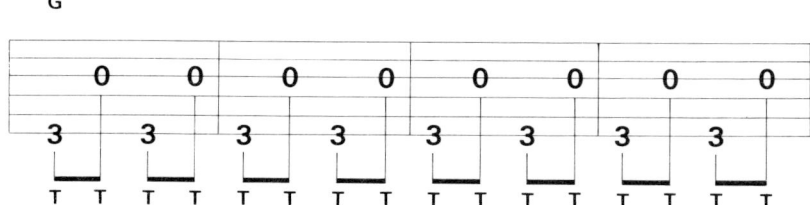

Try it, but don't forget to count the beats.

Do you remember how much more professional the scratch style sounded when you alternated the basses? Look at this:

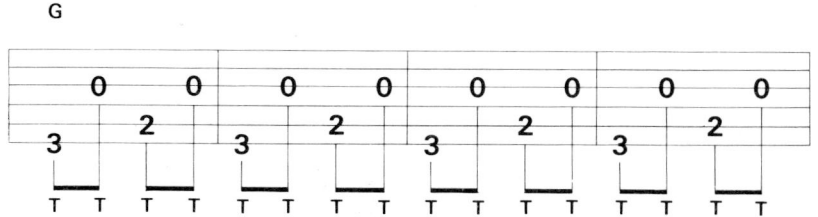

How does that sound to you?

Now try this exercise, but take it slowly.

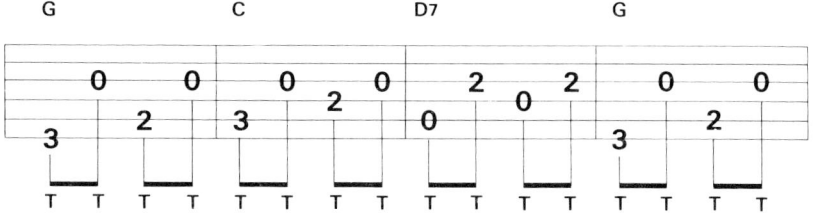

How did you get on with it?

I'd like you to spend some time practicing it until it sounds really smooth. Don't try to race, though. The speed will come when your hands are certain of what they are supposed to play.

PLAYING ON THE BEAT

Now, your rock is composed of four beats or counts:

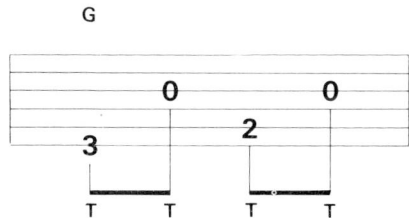

and we can play a simultaneous melody note on any, or all, of these counts.

For example:

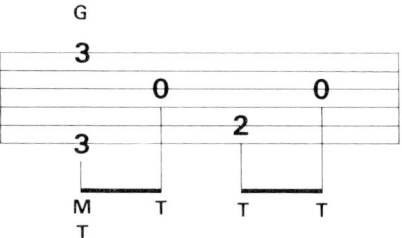

104

Here we have a middle-finger pluck on the first string fretted at the third fret, at the same time as your thumb plucks the first count of the rock on the sixth string.

Try it for yourself, and don't forget to count aloud:

ONE TWO THREE FOUR ONE TWO THREE FOUR etc.

A simultaneous melody note can also be played on count TWO:

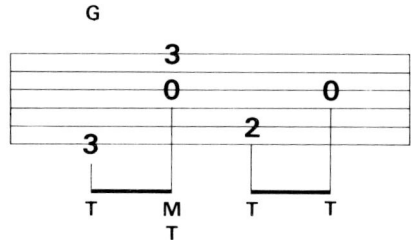

Count THREE:

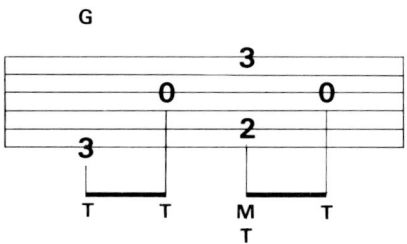

Or count FOUR:

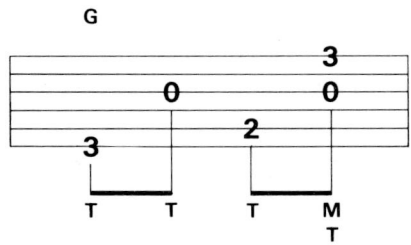

Here is an exercise to familiarize you with the technique. As always, don't try to break any speed records, and count the beats as you play them.

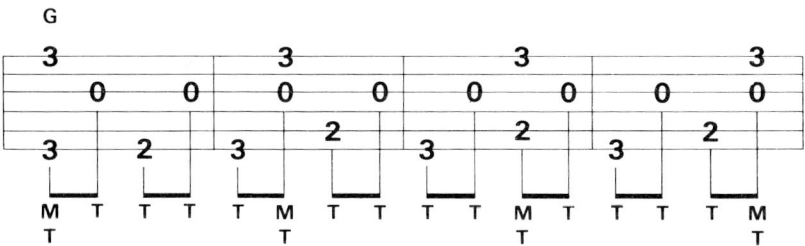

How's it coming along?   Fine.

"AND" COUNTS

Now, as I told you, it is possible to play melody on any, or all, of the rock counts:

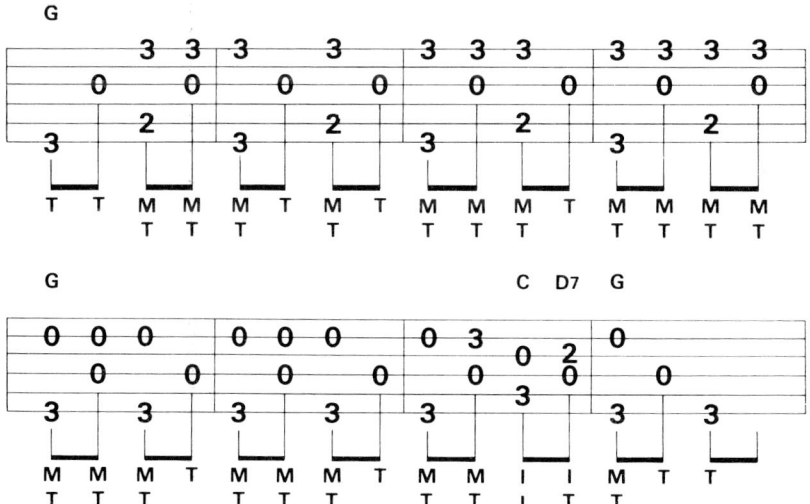

Not so difficult, is it?

However, not all tunes obligingly fall into this even rhythm; many more contain notes which fall between the regular beats in a bar. To play these we resort to "AND" counts.

"AND" counts are simply counts that fall *between* the counts normally played by the thumb.

Here is the basic rock, once more:

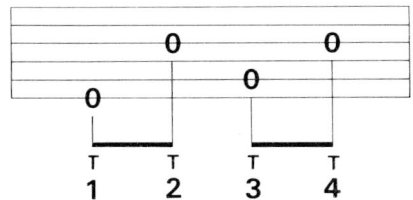

If we play an extra note between count ONE and count TWO:

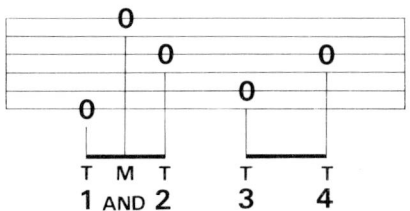

the rhythm would be:

ONE-AND TWO   THREE   FOUR

Hence the name "AND" counts.
follows. First, a line is dropped to the tempo bracket:

"AND" counts are written down as follows. First, a line is dropped to the tempo bracket:

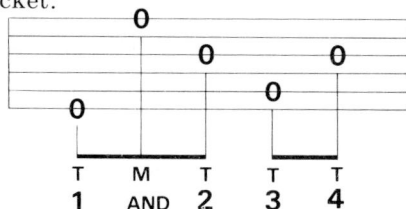

Then the "AND" count is linked to a neighboring note, usually the one before it.

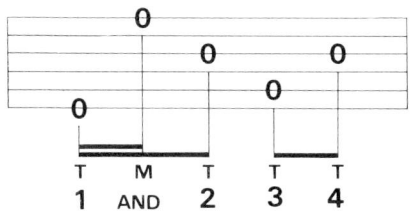

This makes the rhythm:

ONE-AND TWO   THREE   FOUR

You can play "AND" counts between any, or all, of the thumb counts, like this:

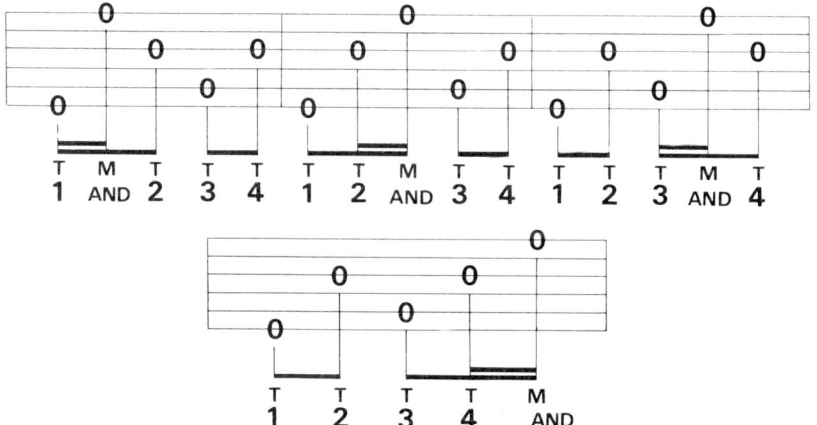

Practice this "AND" count exercise, and take care to keep the thumb-count rhythm regular. For instance it's:

ONE-AND TWO   THREE   FOUR

not

ONE   AND   TWO   THREE   FOUR.

Next is a tune which uses both simultaneous and "AND"-count melody notes.

"FRÈRE JACQUES"

Arr. Pearse

G

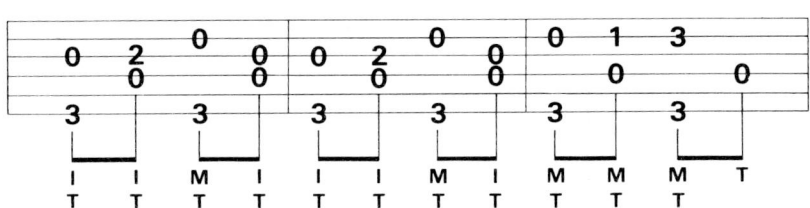

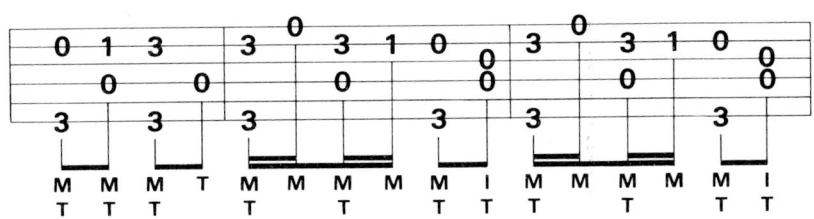

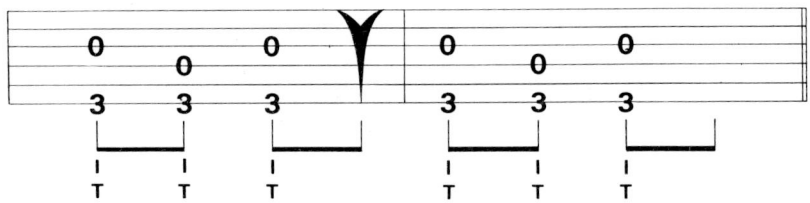

When we are using a rocking-thumb accompaniment it's usual to play the melody notes with just the index and middle finger. This is because in many songs the thumb rocks right over to the third string, so if we had our first finger on the third string, our second on the second string, and our third on the first string, we'd get rather tangled.

With the rocking-thumb technique, most players rest the first finger on the second string, and the second finger on the first string, and pluck any of the three melody strings with whichever finger feels most natural.

Throughout this book, I'll notate fingerings which I find most comfortable. Play them my way first, and then if you want to use different fingerings go right ahead.

Let's look at BAR ONE:

G

```
─────────────────────────────────
              0
   0     2         0
         0         0
─────────────────────────────────
   3         3
─────────────────────────────────

   I     I    M     I
   T     T    T     T
```

Hold down a G chord.

Count ONE	Index finger plucks the open third string, while *simultaneously* the thumb plucks the sixth string held down behind the third fret.
Count TWO	Index finger plucks third string held down behind the second fret (easiest fretting finger, the second), while *sumultaneously* the thumb plucks the open fourth string.
Count THREE	Middle finger plucks the open second string, while *simultaneously* the thumb plucks the sixth string held down behind the third fret.
Count FOUR	The index finger plucks the open third string, while *simultaneously* the thumb plucks the open fourth string.

As always, take it slowly and don't be afraid of making mistakes.

BAR TWO is the same as BAR ONE, so you can already play two bars—how's that for progress?

Let's try BAR THREE:

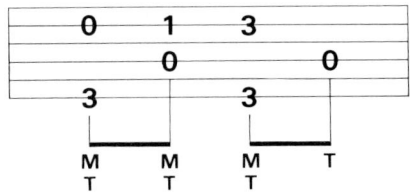

You are still holding down a chord of G.

Count ONE	Middle finger plucks the open second string, while *simultaneously* the thumb plucks the sixth string held down behind the third fret.
Count TWO	Middle finger plucks the second string, held down behind the first fret (easiest fretting finger, the first), while *simultaneously* the thumb plucks the open fourth string.
Count THREE	Middle finger plucks the second string held down behind the third fret (easiest fretting finger, the third), while *simultaneously* the thumb plucks the sixth string held down behind the third fret.
Count FOUR	Thumb plucks the open fourth string, thus completing its rock.

BAR FOUR is the same as BAR THREE, so we'll move on to BAR FIVE:

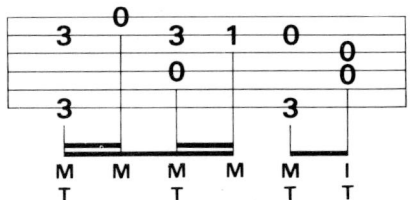

In this bar, we find both simultaneous and "AND" count notes.

The first thing to do is to work out the rhythm. Now we know that any count with a thumb marked on it is likely to be one of the four basic beats.

So any count without a thumb marked on it is probably an "AND" count.

Bearing this in mind, can you work out what the rhythm should be?

That's right, it's:

ONE-AND   TWO-AND   THREE   FOUR

Let's try to play it.

Hold down your chord of G once more.

Count ONE	Middle finger plucks the second string held down behind the third fret (easiest fretting finger, the third), while *simultaneously* the thumb plucks the sixth string held down behind the third fret.
"AND" count	Middle finger plucks the open first string.
Count TWO	Middle finger plucks the second string held down behind the third fret (easiest fretting finger, the third), while *simultaneously* the thumb plucks the open fourth string.
"AND" count	Middle finger plucks the second string held down behind the first fret (easiest fretting finger, the first).
Count THREE	Middle finger plucks the open second string, while *simultaneously* the thumb plucks the sixth string held down behind the third fret.
Count FOUR	Index finger plucks the open third string, while *simultaneously* the thumb plucks the open fourth string.

Remember, the rhythm is:

ONE-AND   TWO-AND   THREE   FOUR

BAR SIX is the same as BAR FIVE.

In BARS SEVEN and EIGHT,

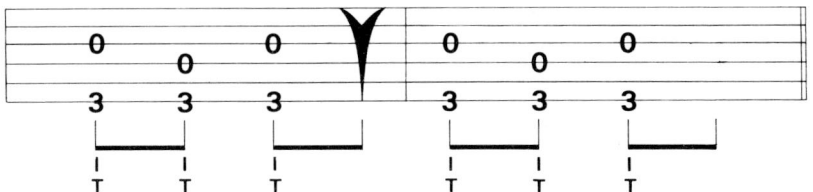

there are two things to watch out for. The first is that the rock is dropped in favor of a drone bass on the sixth string; and the other is that no finger is marked under the brush stroke. This is because, unless specifically marked, brush strokes are normally played with the *middle finger*. Apart from these points, the last two bars of the tune are quite easy, so I'll leave you to try them for yourself.

Did you manage them?

Good.

Now go back to the beginning and practice the tune over until it sounds relaxed and confident.

A NEW KEY-C MAJOR

A very useful key for melody playing is the key of C major. Here are the three main chords:

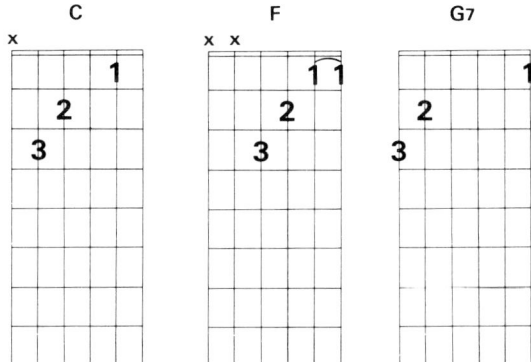

You can already play the chord of C, so we'll move on to the second chord in the sequence, the chord of F.

This is one of the most awkward chords to finger, because, like the chord of A7, it requires that you hold down more than one string with your first finger.

The first finger lays across the first two strings, just behind the first fret.

The second finger holds down the third string, just behind the second fret.

The third finger holds down the fourth string, just behind the third fret.

The fifth and sixth strings are silent.

Here's how it looks:

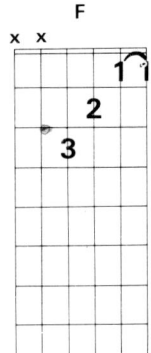

Now hold down the chord of F and pluck each string in turn, starting with the first string.

How does the chord sound? If the first string sounds muffled, push down against the fingerboard with the first joint of your finger, flattening it against the string. It should sound better now.

Don't worry if you can't get a good sound right away. The chord of F is a stumbling block for everyone learning guitar.

When each of the four strings sounds clear and unmuffled, you can try adding on a sixth string bass note. To accomplish this, we hold down the sixth string just behind the first fret, with the left-hand thumb.

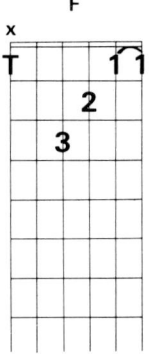

It's not necessary to include the sixth string in the chord, but if you can manage to get your thumb around the neck onto the string, it gives you a very useful bass note to include in your rock.

Try it. It'll take a good deal of perseverence, but it's well worth the effort.

If, after a great deal of effort, you still find the stretch quite impossible because your hands are too small, don't despair; just return your thumb to its normal resting place behind the neck, and remember not to play on either the sixth or fifth strings when you're playing the chord.

Now for a really easy chord (almost anything would be easier after F!): the chord of G7.

G7

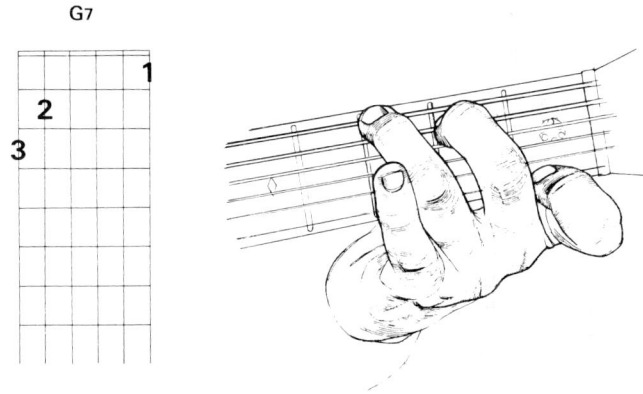

First finger holds down the first string just behind the first fret.

Second finger holds down the fifth string just behind the second fret.

Third finger holds down the sixth string just behind the third fret.

When you can change from chord to chord easily — not before — try this next tune.

"AUNT RHODIE"

Arr. Pearse

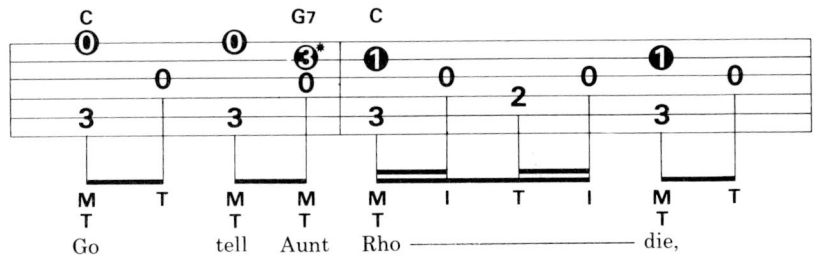

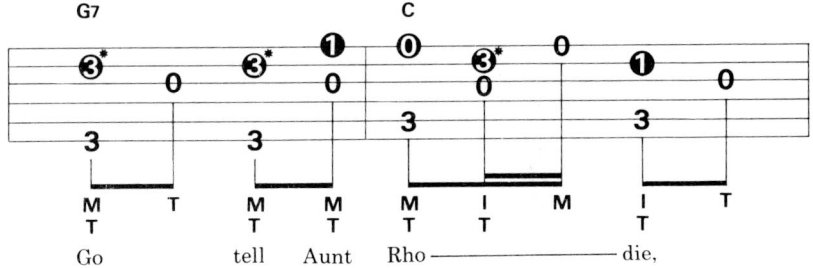

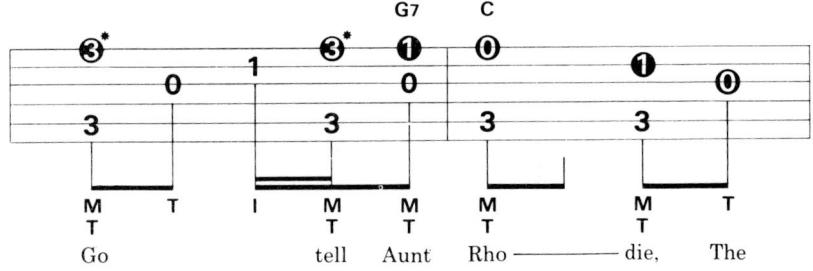

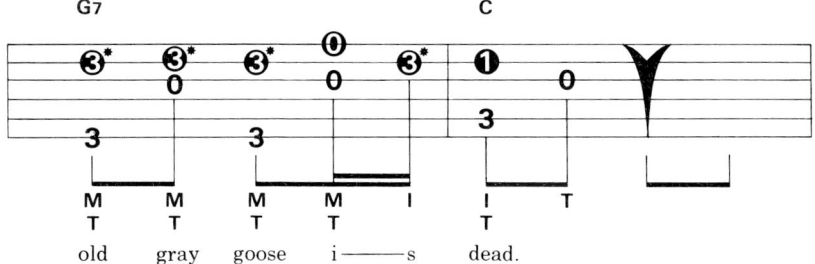

old   gray   goose   i———s   dead.

The one that she's been saving,
The one that she's been saving,
The one that she's been saving,
To make a feather bed.

It drownded in the mill pond,
It drownded in the mill pond,
It drownded in the mill pond,
A-standing on its head.

The goslings are a-crying,
The goslings are a-crying,
The goslings are a-crying,
Because their mama's dead.

So, go tell Aunt Rhodie,
Go tell Aunt Rhodie,
Go tell Aunt Rhodie,
The old gray goose is dead.

Remember, before you start to play any piece of tablature, go through it and work out the rhythm of each bar. To help you this time, I'll give you a rhythm breakdown:

1 2 3 4 │ 1– AND 2– AND 3 4 │ 1 2 3 4 │ 1 2– AND 3 4│

1 2 AND –3 4 │ 1...3 4 │ 1 2 3 4– AND │ 1 2 3 ...

As a further guide, in case you haven't heard the song before, I've ringed the actual notes of the melody, so that they stand out from the accompaniment. So, let's try BAR ONE together:

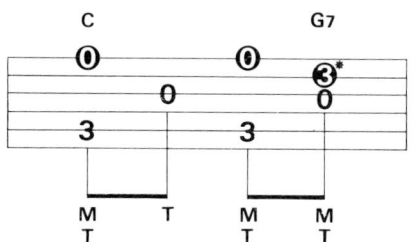

Hold down a chord of C.

    Count ONE   Middle finger plucks the open first string, while *simultaneously* the thumb plucks the fifth string held down behind the third fret.

    Count TWO   Thumb plucks the open third string.

    Count THREE   Middle finger plucks the open first string, while *simultaneously* the thumb plucks the fifth string held down behind the third fret.

Hold down a chord of G7.

    Count FOUR   Middle finger plucks the second string held down behind the third fret (the asterisk * tells us that the easiest finger to fret with is the *fourth*, so every time you see a note that is marked * use the *fourth* finger to hold it down), while *simultaneously* the thumb plucks the open third string.

Try it on your own.

Not so difficult, is it?

BAR TWO

Without looking at the rhythm breakdown that I gave you, can you work out the rhythm of BAR TWO? Take your time; remember the trick lies in recognizing the basic beats. These are played by the thumb, so any notes which don't fall on a thumb count are most likely to be "AND" counts.

So what would you say the rhythm of the next bar was?

That's right:

ONE-AND   TWO-AND   THREE   FOUR

Let's play it through together.

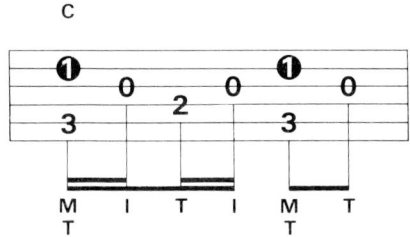

Hold down a C chord.

Count ONE	Middle finger plucks the second string held down behind the first fret, while *simultaneously* the thumb plucks the fifth string held down behind the third fret.
"AND" count	Index finger plucks the open third string.
Count TWO	Thumb plucks the fourth string held down behind the second fret.
"AND" count	Index finger plucks the open third string.
Count THREE	Middle finger plucks the second string held down behind the first fret, while *simultaneously* the thumb plucks the fifth string held down behind the third fret.
Count FOUR	Thumb plucks the open third string.

OK, now go back to the start of the song and play through as far as we've gone. It's very important that each bar follows on from the preceding one without any hesitation. To help you develop this fluidity, try singing along as you play. As ever, keep the tempo nice and easy. Just relax. If you're relaxed, your playing will sound relaxed too.

Now hold down a chord of G7, and we'll play through BAR THREE:

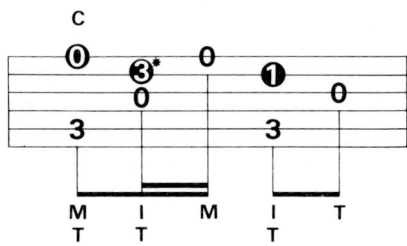

Count ONE	Middle finger plucks the second string held down behind the third fret (by the fourth finger . . . remember the asterisk?), while *simultaneously* the thumb plucks the sixth string held down behind the third fret.
Count TWO	Thumb plucks the open third string.
Count THREE	Middle finger plucks the second string, held down behind the third fret (asterisk * !), while *simultaneously* the thumb plucks the sixth string held down behind the third fret.
Count FOUR	Middle finger plucks the first string held down behind the first fret, while *simultaneously* the thumb plucks the open third string.

BAR FOUR

Hold down a chord of C.

Count ONE	Middle finger plucks the open first string, while *simultaneously* the thumb plucks the fifth string held down behind the third fret.
Count TWO	Index finger plucks the second string held down behind third fret (remember what * means?), while *simultaneously* the thumb plucks the open third string.
"AND" count	Middle finger plucks the open first string.
Count THREE	Index finger plucks the second string held down behind the first fret, while *simultaneously* the thumb plucks the fifth string held down behind the third fret.
Count FOUR	Thumb plucks the open third string.

How are you getting along?

Well, we're halfway through the tune so it would be advisable now to play through what we've done so far, just to make sure it's all linking together smoothly. Believe me, the care you take now will determine just how good a guitarist you become.

Only when you're quite satisfied with the sound of the first four bars should you move on.

OK, here's BAR FIVE:

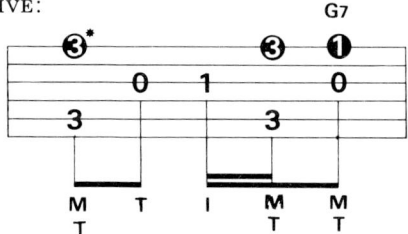

Can you see something unusual about the rhythm?

That's right, the "AND" count is linked to the *following* count, rather than the one before it. This makes the rhythm:

ONE   TWO   AND-THREE   FOUR.

Right! Hold down a chord of C once more.

Count ONE	Middle finger plucks the first string held down behind the third fret (* !), while *simultaneously* the thumb plucks the sixth string held down behind the third fret.
Count TWO	Thumb plucks the open third string.
"AND" count	Index finger plucks the second string held down behind the first fret.
Count THREE	Middle finger plucks the first string held down behind the third fret (* !), while *simultaneously* the thumb plucks the fifth string held down behind the third fret.

Change to a chord of G7.

Count FOUR	Middle finger plucks the first string held down behind first fret, while *simultaneously* the thumb plucks the open third string.

You shouldn't have had too much trouble with that bar, but when you practice it, make certain that you do get the rhythm correct. It's:

ONE   TWO   AND-THREE   FOUR

not

ONE   TWO-AND   THREE   FOUR

The next bar, BAR SIX, is one for you to play on your own. Just remember to make a pause on count TWO.

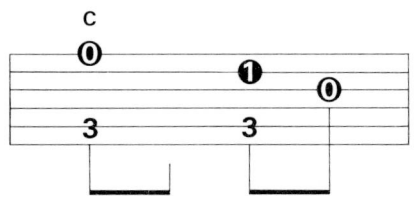

ONE . . . THREE FOUR

. . . and so to BAR SEVEN:

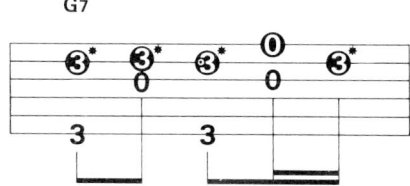

Hold down a chord of G7.

Count ONE   Middle finger plucks the second string held down behind the third fret (* !), while *simultaneously* the thumb plucks the sixth string held down behind the third fret.

Count TWO   Middle finger plucks the second string held down behind the third fret (* !), while *simultaneously* the thumb plucks the open third string.

Count THREE   Middle finger plucks the second string held down behind the third fret (* !), while *simultaneously* the thumb plucks the sixth string held down behind the third fret.

Count FOUR   Middle finger plucks the open first string (remove first finger from chord fingering), while *simultaneously* the thumb plucks the open third string.

"AND" count   Index finger plucks the second string held down behind the third fret (* !).

OK?

I'm going to leave the last bar, BAR EIGHT, to you.

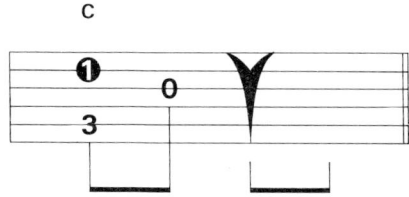

Although it's technically very simple to play, make sure that you do get the rhythm right. When you've got a silent count in a bar, it's very easy to go wrong.

The rhythm is:

ONE   TWO   THREE   · · ·

This may seem a very obvious thing to point out, but you'll be surprised how many people make it sound like:

ONE AND TWO

By the way, you do remember what finger to play the brush with, don't you?

THE KEY OF A MINOR

How about another key? This time it's a minor key—the key of A minor, which is the relative minor to the key of C major.

Here are the three main chords:

By now, you should have no difficulty working out the fingering of a new chord. Take your time, though, and don't skimp the practice.

You're now at a stage when because of a growing confidence in your ability to make music on the guitar, you may have a strong temptation to rush through irksome things, like learning new chords, in order to get to a new style or song. Make sure, therefore, that you practice everything that I show you before you move on.

"THE TREADMILL"

Arr. Pearse

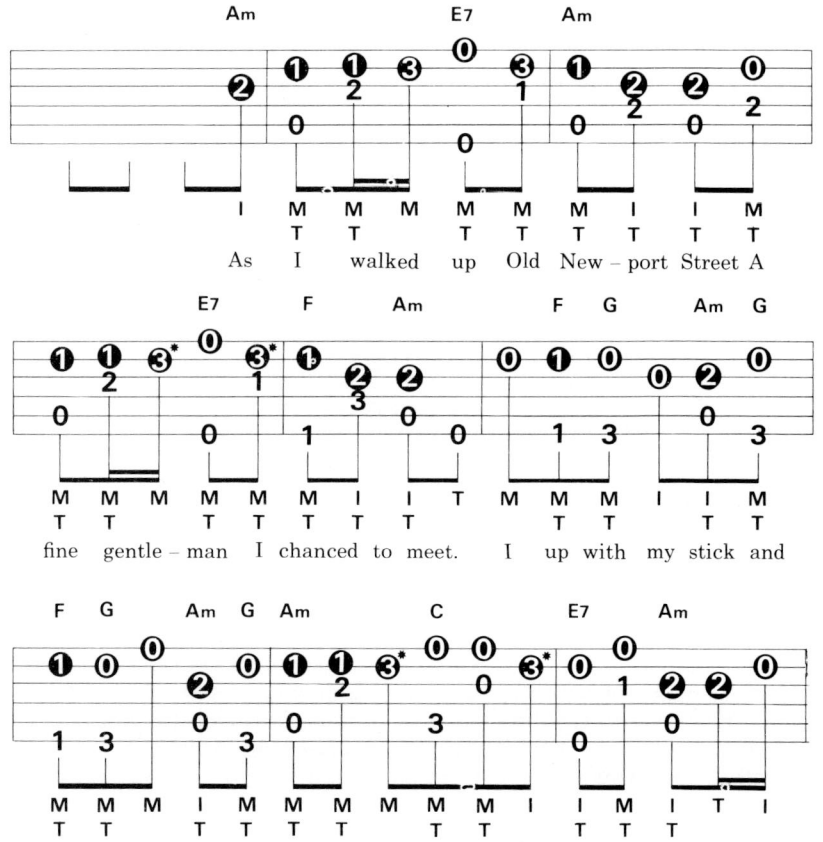

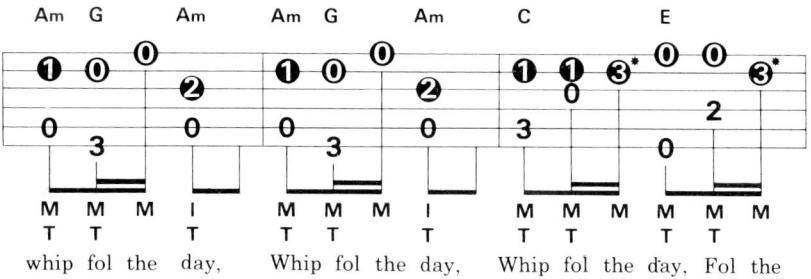

whip fol the day, Whip fol the day, Whip fol the day, Fol the

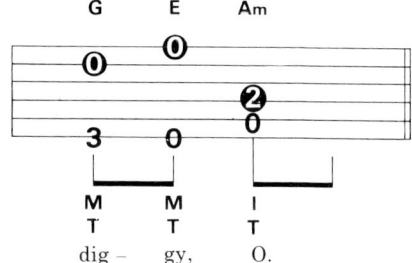

dig – gy, O.

As I walked up Old Newport Street
A fine gentleman I chanced to meet.
I up with my stick and knocked him down
And out of his pocket I stole five pound.

    To my whip fol the day
    Whip fol the day
    Whip fol the day,
    Fol the diggy, O.

I lay in the guard house all that night
Till eight o'clock of the morning, O.
Then they brought me up before Mr. Hook
And in this black book he did look.

"Step up, young man, I know your face.
That's nothing in your favor.
Some little time I'll give to you
Six months unto hard labor."

At five o'clock the turnkey comes round.
I think they calls him Mr. Grimes.
We leaves our cells without a sound
And tread the wheel till breakfast time.

At eight o'clock the bell does chime
And it's into the chapel for praying time.
Down on our bended knees we fall.
Oh, Lord, have mercy on us all.

Then at nine o'clock it's back to work,
And it's Heaven help the lads who shirk.
It's tread the track till suppertime,
The wheel to turn and the corn to grind.

But now my time is up and past
And I can return to my home at last.
I'll leave my mates with Mr. Grimes,
The wheel to turn and the corn to grind.

This is a song from the days when prisoners were made to walk the treadmill in English jails. Although that practice is thankfully no longer with us, "The Treadmill" is still known and sung all over England.

For this guitar arrangement I've tried to capture the feeling of the endless circle in which the prisoners were condemned to walk.

As always, let's take a look at the rhythm before we start.

First BAR ONE:

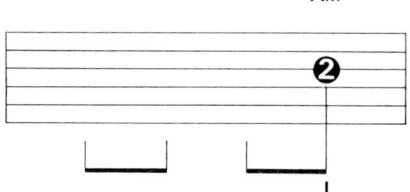

This is quite interesting because it contains only one note, and even though it isn't played by the thumb, it is one of the basic four counts. You see, although you can say in most cases any thumb pluck will be one of the basic counts in a bar, there are many occasions when one or more counts are carried by a finger on its own.

To simplify it then: in rocking thumb techniques, thumb plucks normally occur on the basic counts in a bar. Finger plucks, without a simultaneous thumb pluck, normally occur on "AND" counts. You will also come across basic counts played solely by finger plucks. However, you will seldom come across "AND" counts played by the thumb.

OK, so just one note in BAR ONE, and that occurs on count FOUR.

The other bars are uncomplicated, but just in case you are still uncertain I'll set out the rhythm of each bar before we start.

   · · · 4 | 1 2–AND 3 4 | 1 2 3 4 | 1 2–AND 3 4 |

1 2 3 4 AND |–1 2–AND 3 4 | 1 2–AND 3 4 | 1 2– AND –3 4– AND|

1 2 3 4 AND | 1 2–AND 3 · · · | 1 2–AND 3 · · · | 1 2–AND 3 4 |

1 2 3 · · ·

As I think it's time you became more self-reliant, I'll just take you through the first three bars, and then leave you on your own.

Hold down a chord of A minor.

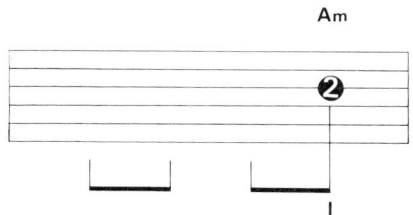

Count FOUR   Index finger plucks the third string held
              down behind the second fret.

BAR TWO

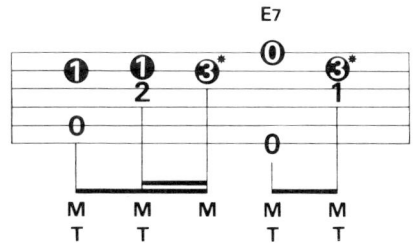

Still hold down a chord of A minor.

Count ONE   Middle finger plucks the second string held
              down behind the first fret, while
              simultaneously the thumb plucks the open
              fifth string.

Count TWO   Middle finger plucks the second string held
              down behind the first fret, while
              simultaneously the thumb plucks the third
              string held down behind the second fret.

"AND" count   Middle finger plucks the second string held
              down behind the third fret (* !).

Now, change to a chord of E7.

Count THREE   Middle finger plucks the open first string, while *simultaneously* the thumb plucks the open sixth string.

Count FOUR   Middle finger plucks the second string held down behind the third fret (* !), while *simultaneously* the thumb plucks the third string held down behind the first fret.

Am

BAR THREE

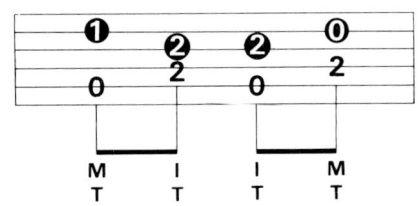

Change back to a chord of A minor.

Count ONE   Middle finger plucks the second string held down behind the first fret, while *simultaneously* the thumb plucks the open fifth string.

Count TWO   Index finger plucks the third string held down behind the second fret, while *simultaneously* the thumb plucks the fourth string, held down behind the second fret.

Count THREE   Index finger plucks the third string held down behind the second fret, while *simultaneously* the thumb plucks the open fifth string.

Count FOUR   Middle finger plucks the open second string, while *simultaneously* the thumb plucks the fourth string held down behind the second fret.

How are you getting on?

Now go through the rest of the tune, remembering to practice each bar with the one before it as you go.

Take your time, and don't worry.

Did you get through it?

OK, now go back to the beginning and practice.

THE CAPO-AND HOW TO USE IT

You've probably discovered as you move from tune to tune that it's easier for you to sing songs in some keys than in others. Even opera singers have certain keys which they favor, and conversely keys which they try to avoid, because their voices sound, for instance, too "reedy" in the upper register or too quiet in the lower. For us ordinary mortals, therefore, life can get rather depressing if we come across a song arrangement in a key quite unsuited to our voice.

I always have trouble with the key of G, for instance. Any song in that key always seems to be just a little too high or a little too low. This is unfortunate because the chords in that key—G, C and so on —lend themselves to attractive finger-style accompaniments.

One way to solve the problem is to use a CAPO.

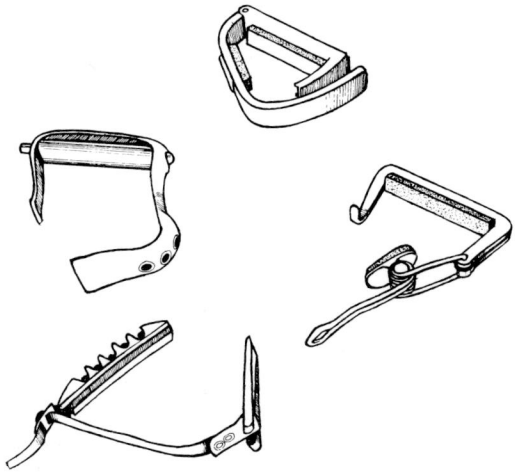

The capo is a mechanical device which raises the pitch of all six strings on your guitar uniformly. It operates on the principle that we were talking about right at the very start of the book—that each fret raised the pitch of a string a halftone.

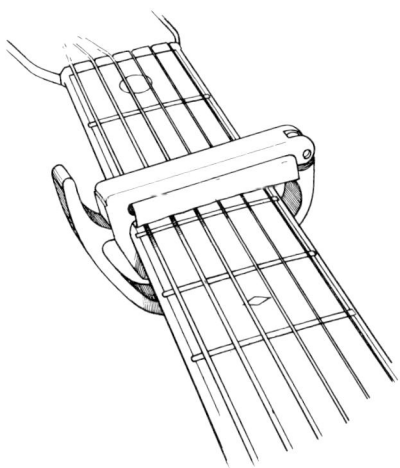

For example, say you're accompanying a song in the key of C and you find that the key is too low for you to sing it comfortably. If you attach the capo to the fingerboard just behind the first fret and play your C chords, the sound that you produce will be one halftone higher—C♯.

If you put the capo on at the second fret, you'll be playing in D, and so on in halftones up the fingerboard.

It's just the same as playing a GRAND BARRE, with one finger right the way across all the strings.

Now, there are many different types of capo; in fact they date back to the earliest fretted instruments. From carvings we know that the Egyptians and the Moors used capos, apparently made from sinew or twine, which they bound tightly about the necks of their instruments. The cittern family—of which the only two surviving members are the Thuringer waldzither and the Portuguese gitarre —employed a "bolt and nut" style capo, which clamped down through a hole in the neck. The position marks on the fingerboards of modern guitars are the vestigial remains of this practice.

Here is a capo position table which I have set out for you:

CHORDS IN THE KEY OF

	A	B	C	D	E	F	G
At the 1st fret	B♭	C	C♯	E♭	F	F♯	A♭
2nd	B	C♯	D	E	F♯	G	A
3rd	C	D	E♭	F	G	A♭	B♭
4th	C♯	E♭	E	F♯	A♭	A	B
5th	D	E	F	G	A	B♭	C
6th	E♭	F	F♯	A♭	B♭	B	C♯
7th	E	F♯	G	A	B	C	D
8th	F	G	A♭	B♭	C	C♯	E♭
9th	F♯	A♭	A	B	C♯	D	E
10th	G	A	B♭	C	D	E♭	F
11th	A♭	B♭	B	C♯	E♭	E	F♯
12th	A	B	C	D	E	F	G

This is how it works: if you want to play in the key of C, for instance, you could capo at the third fret and play in A, or capo at the tenth fret and play the chords of D, or capo at the eighth fret and play in E. You will also be playing in C if you capo at the seventh fret and play in F, or at the fifth fret and play in the key of G. All of these will produce the sound of the key of C.

Well, here we are at the end of Part I. You got through it.

Congratulations!

With the learning of any instrument, the most difficult time is right at the start, forcing your unwilling fingers into strange and often painful positions and having to keep so much new information at the front of your mind all the time. Naturally, as time goes by, this information fits itself into the background, becoming automatic and instinctive. This is the stage that you should now be approaching.

Of course, you should still have to think about what you're playing. If the whole thing becomes automatic, then so will your music. But your hands should now be remembering chord fingering, and the thumb rock should be almost playing itself, allowing you to give more attention to the real business of playing and interpretation. In the words of the old song: "It ain't what you do, it's the way that you do it."

THE
SONG AND SOLO
SECTION

PLAYING YOUR WAY

Never be content with playing the tune in exactly the same way that it was taught to you. Once you're sure that you understand the rhythms and fingerings set out in my arrangement of a tune, try to modify it, making it something which is personal to you. A great deal can be done in the early stages by careful use of light and shade, and slight tempo changes. By this I mean that you should go through each tune asking yourself the following questions: should the notes in this part of the tune:

(a) be slightly louder?

(b) be slightly softer?

(c) be slightly harder?

(d) be slightly more mellow?

(e) be dampened?

(f) be anticipated?

(g) be hesitated?

(h) be played straight?

(i) be played with vibrato?

Some of these effects are self-evident, others need more explanation; I'll deal with these in turn.

(a) and (b): Well these should be obvious. If you pick or scratch a string hard, the note it produces will be much louder than if you just stroke it gently. When playing loudly, however, it's not a good idea to play so hard that the strings bounce against the fingerboard frets as this produces a rather ugly sound.

(c) and (d): The closer to the bridge that you pluck or scratch a string, the sharper and more metallic will be its tone. The closer to the fingerboard end that you pluck or scratch a string, the mellower will be the tone.

(e): There are two main ways by which you may damp a string to prevent its ringing on too long:

> 1. *Left-hand damping:* If you want to damp a string which is being held down by a left-hand finger, just relax that finger slightly, letting the natural springiness of the string push your fingertip slightly away from the fingerboard. As this happens, the note will die. Try it.

> This is also a very useful way of damping a whole chord. You just relax your whole left-hand grip very slightly.

> 2. *Right-hand damping:* A very effective method of damping with the right hand is to rest the edge of the hand, below the base of the little finger, across the bridge saddle, damping either all of the strings or just the bass strings.

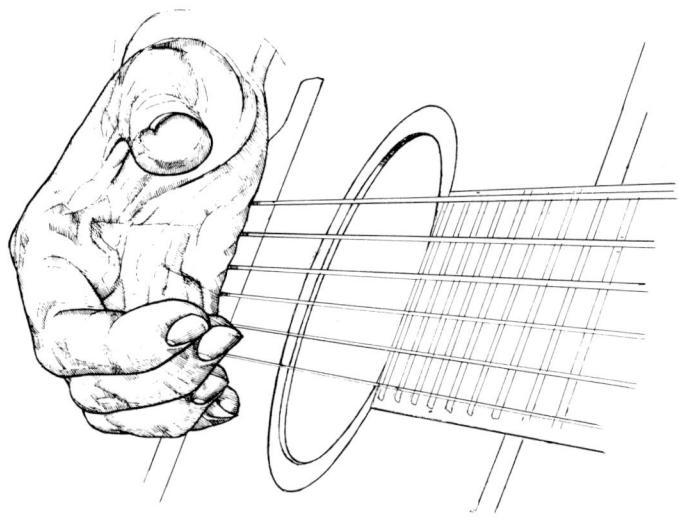

Nashville guitar stylists play with this hand attitude much of the time because it gives them a "chunky," muffled bass rock, but I tend to think that if used too often, it can lead to a player developing a rather cramped hand attitude.

(f) and (g): When you're playing a melody you should always ask yourself whether or not certain notes might have a greater impact or improve the flow of the tune if you were to play them slightly earlier or later than you would normally. This anticipation, or hesitation, must always be very discreetly and subtly used if it's not to sound like bad coordination. Used with thought, however, it can transform an arrangement. In a tune containing a rocking bass count, this variation is best applied only to the finger-plucked notes, the bass rock remaining constant. Instead of plucking a melody note simultaneously with a bass, the finger plucks it either a fraction of a second before, or a fraction after, the thumb count. Now, this takes a lot of practice to get the sound just right—but believe me, it's more than worth it.

(h) and (i): So far every note which you've played has been played straight; that is, the string has been plucked or scratched either open or held down by a finger of the left hand. This produces a good tone, but the tone tends to die away rather quickly. In order to prolong or sustain the note we use VIBRATO.

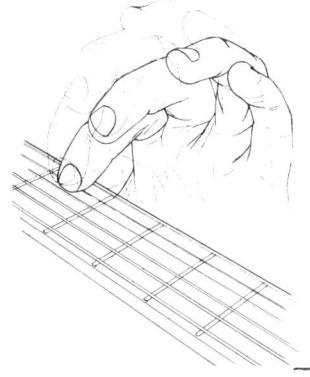

When a string has been plucked, the fretting finger is gently rocked to and fro along the axis of the string.

This raises and relaxes the string tension, setting up a wave form which intensifies the note, and also tends to make it carry further. To illustrate what I mean, get someone sitting across the room from you to gently sing *Aaaaaaaaaaaaaah*, and then at the same quiet level sing *Yayayayayayayaya*.

The second example will be much more clearly heard, because it's been overlaid with a wave form, and this effect is most useful when applied to slow-moving melodies.

Here are a number of tunes which adapt well to being played on the guitar, and which lend themselves to personalization. All of them are well within your capabilities, but I hope that this doesn't mean that you'll find them too easy. If you always play easy pieces, you'll never be a good guitar player—so I have arranged them with two thoughts in mind. First, each has to stretch your technique slightly; and second, they all have to be good, performable arrangements.

Learn and master each one before you move on to the next, and don't worry—you *can* play each one. Anything that I feel may throw you, I'll explain as you get to it, and any chords or unusual left-hand fingerings will be shown by both a chord window and a picture.

"THE SQUIRREL IS A PRETTY THING"

Arr. Pearse

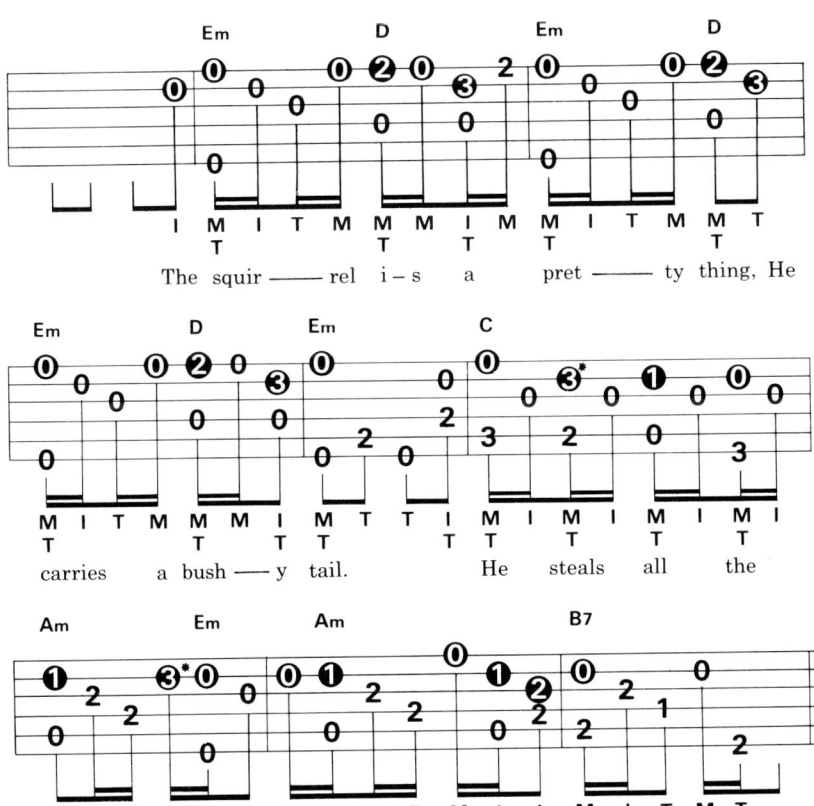

The squirrel is a pretty thing,
He carries a bushy tail.
He steals all the farmer's corn,
And husks it on the rail.

The hawk he is a wily bird,
Wily in the sky.
If he gets in my chicken coop,
He'll make the feathers fly.

The raccoon's tail is ringed around,
Possum's tail goes bare,
Rabbit don't have a tail at all,
Just a bitty bunch of hair.

When I was a little boy
'Bout eighteen inches high,
Thought I heard a jay-bird say,
"You'll marry by and by."

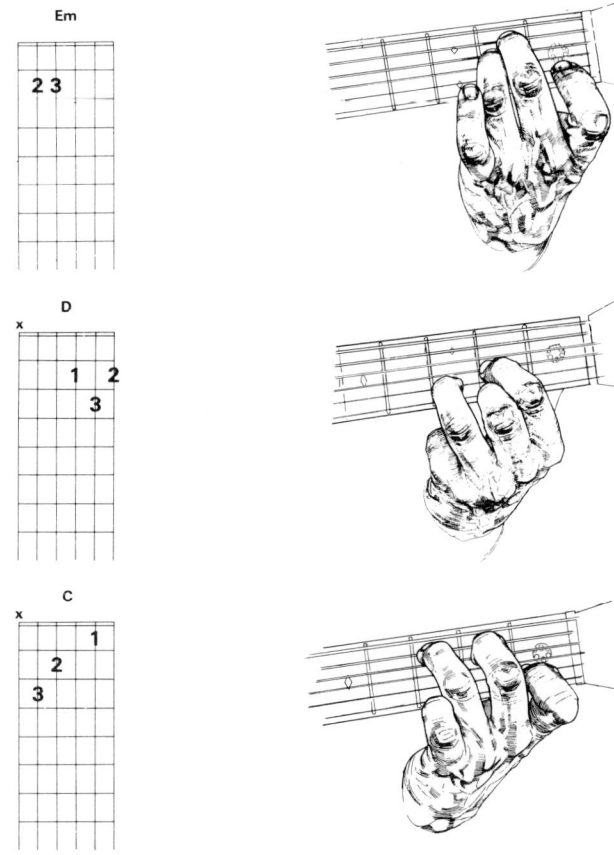

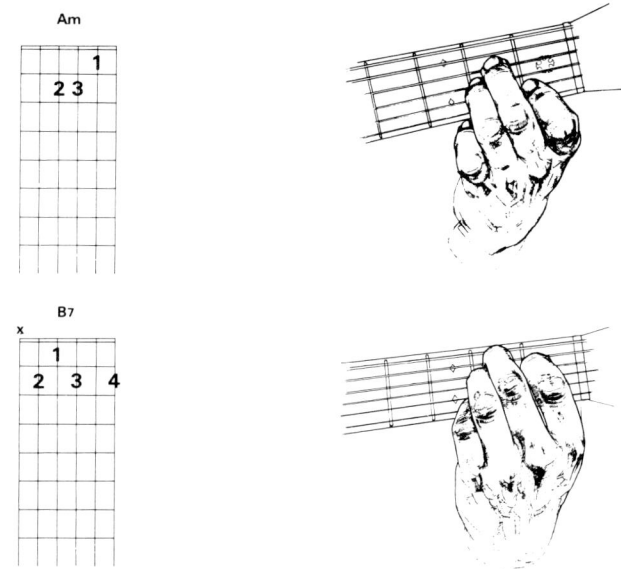

Am

B7

Well, how did you get on?

Not so difficult is it? At least, not if you take the trouble to read
each bar before you try to play it. It only takes a second or two,
just a quick glance through, to sort out the rhythm, to see how the
chord changes are played and, most of all, to discover any pitfalls,
awkward fingerings, etcetera, before you get to them.

It's a lot easier to puzzle out a problem when you're not actually in
the middle of a playing sequence. If you're trying to remember a
new chord shape, sing along at the same time and have your mind
full of subconscious rhythm counting, you're bound to get into hot
water. So before you charge in, take a quiet moment to read through
the tune, bar by bar.

Let's look at the tablature for "Squirrel," then, to see anything that might have given you difficulty.

BAR ONE

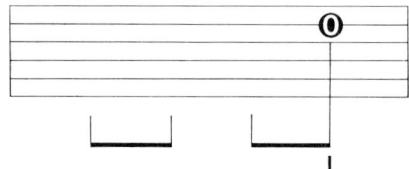

Just one note here, but what is it? Well, it's played by an index-finger pluck, so it could be an "AND" count. But *is* it? It's not joined to a neighboring note, because there *are* no neighboring notes, so that can't help us.

Look at the beat bracket, however; it's just an ordinary simple bracket, so it must be a fourth count then. We'll move on.

BAR TWO

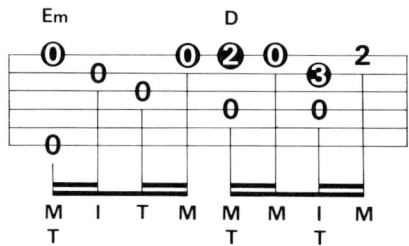

Do you know the rhythm?

It's ONE-AND TWO-AND THREE-AND FOUR-AND.

It looks rather daunting, doesn't it? However, now that you know the rhythm, you can pick out the melody, using the circled notes, and learn how the tune sounds.

If you have the basic melody in your head, the weaving of an accompaniment around it is much easier.

Another tip: once you've worked out and played through a bar, it's quite a good idea to look for similarities in other bars. BAR FOUR, for instance, is exactly the same as BAR TWO. Do you see any other similar bars — or parts of bars?

BAR SIX contains a very attractive progression, the bass notes of which provide a counterpoint to the melody. Again the actual playing shouldn't throw you, but make sure that you let those sonorous bass notes come out loud and clear.

"PAPER OF PINS"

Arr. Pearse

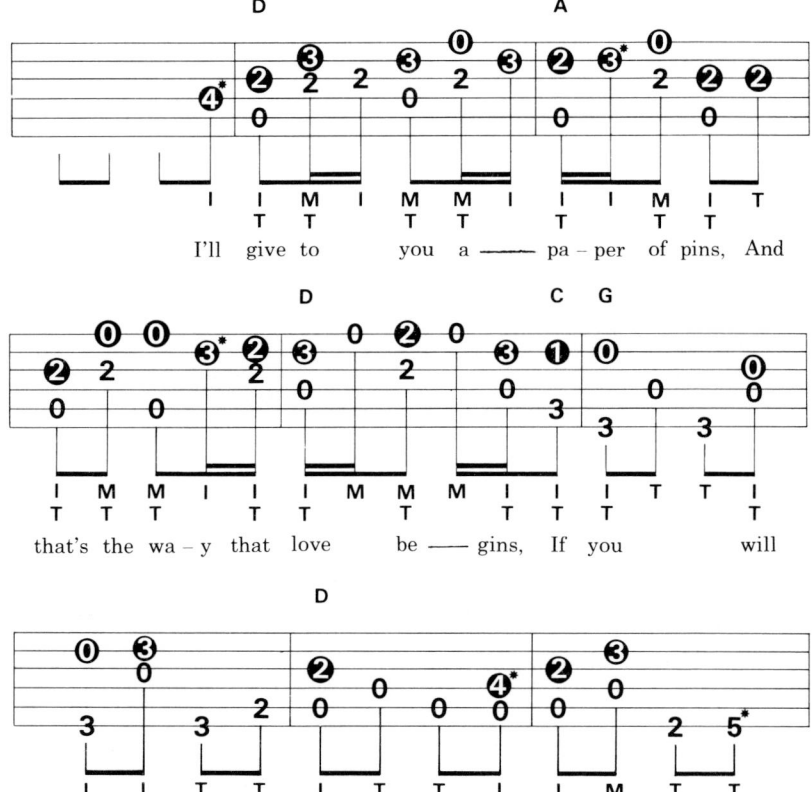

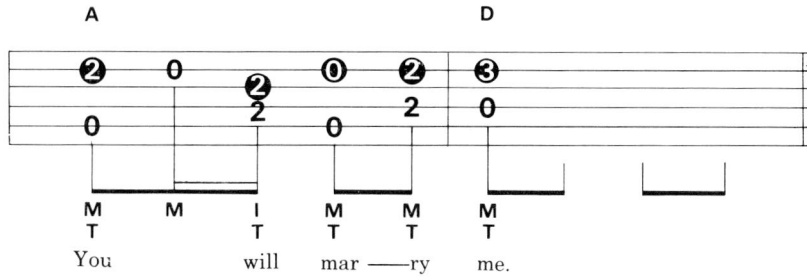

I'll give to you a paper of pins,
And that's the way that love begins,
If you will marry,
You will marry,
You will marry me.

I'll not accept your paper of pins.
That's not the way my love begins.
And I'll not marry,
I'll not marry,
I'll not marry you.

I'll give to you the keys to my heart
That we may marry and never part,
If you will marry,
You will marry,
You will marry me.

I'll not accept the keys to your heart
That we may marry and never part.
And I'll not marry,
I'll not marry,
I'll not marry you.

I'll give to you a golden ball
To bounce from the kitchen to the hall,
If you will marry,
You will marry,
You will marry me.

I'll not accept your golden ball
To bounce from the kitchen to the hall.
And I'll not marry,
I'll not marry,
I'll not marry you.

I'll give to you the keys to my chest
And all the money that I possess.
If you will marry,
You will marry,
You will marry me.

Oh, I'll accept the keys to your chest
And all the money that you possess.
And, yes, I'll marry,
Yes, I'll marry,
Yes, I'll marry you.

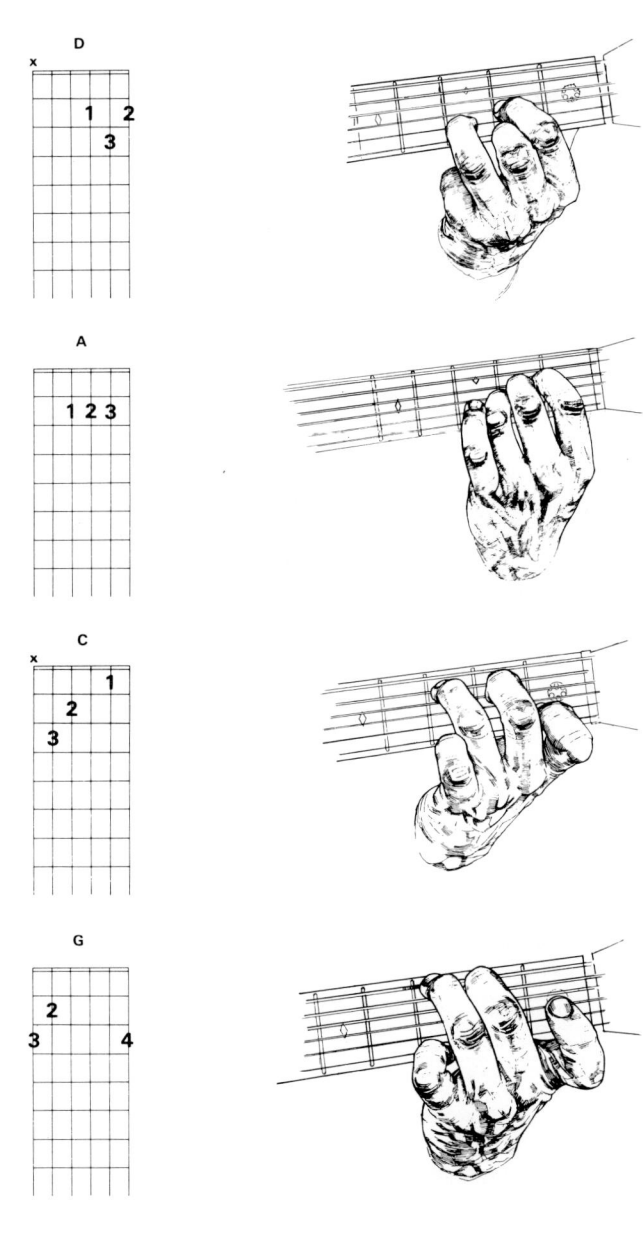

The only bars which you just might have had difficulty with would probably be BARS EIGHT AND NINE.

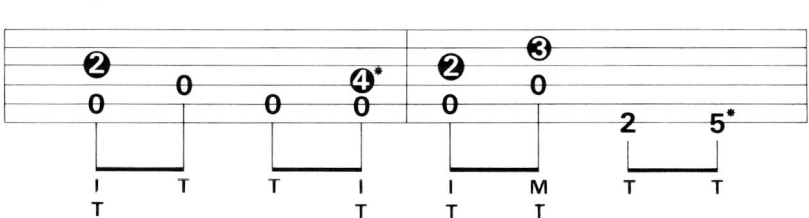

On count FOUR of both bars, your fourth finger has to stretch quite a way in order to reach the required note. If this is too painful at present, don't force it. Leave it for a while, then come back and try it again later on when your fingers have had a chance to recover. By the way, some of my guitar students like to add a brush stroke on count THREE of the last bar, BAR ELEVEN.

Try it. It sounds OK.

"TAILOR AND THE MOUSE"

Arr. Pearse

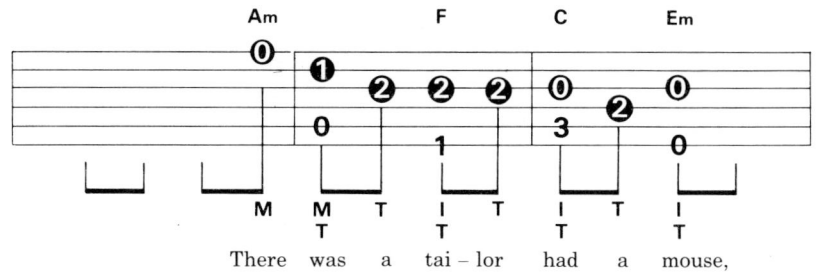

There was a tai – lor had a mouse,

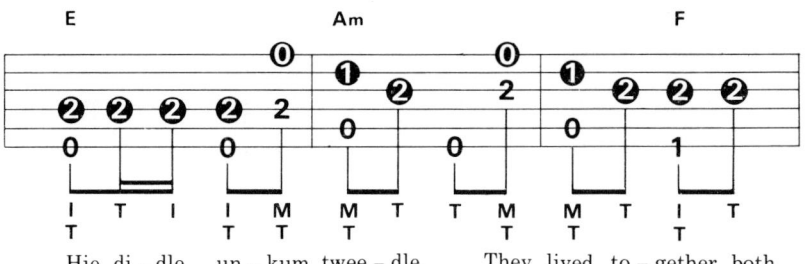

Hie di – dle un – kum twee – dle. They lived to – gether both

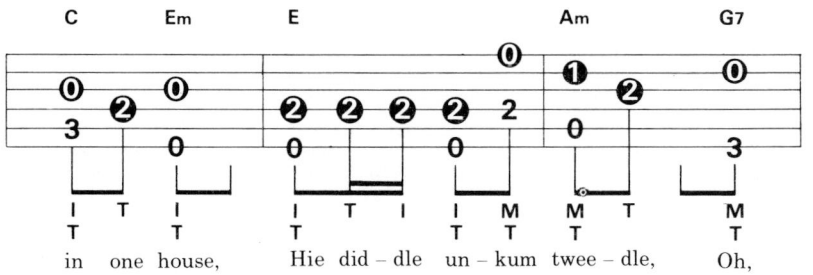

in one house, Hie did – dle un – kum twee – dle, Oh,

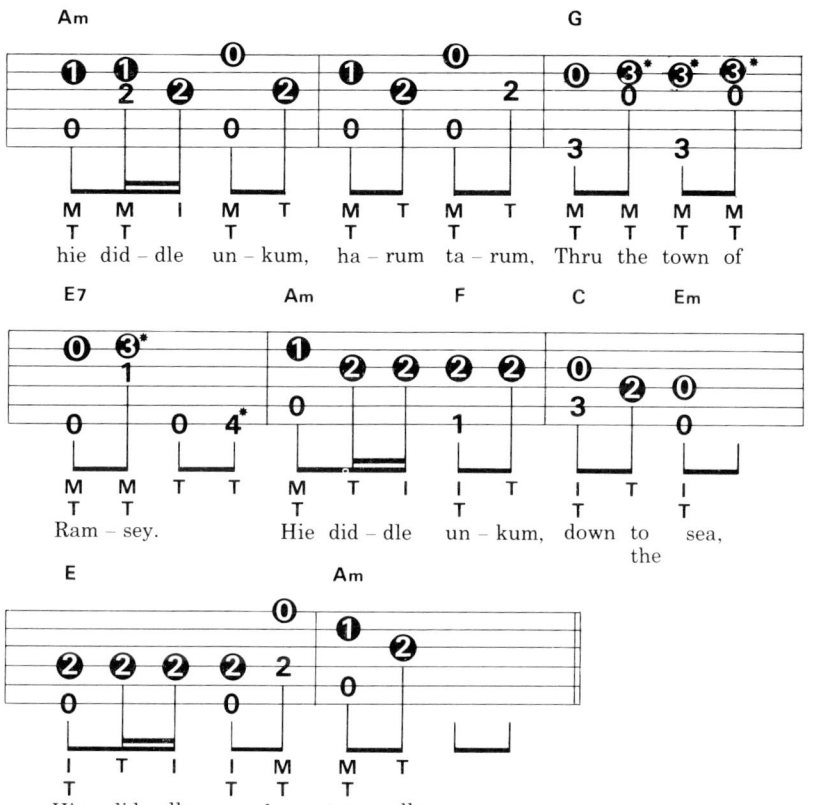

They both slept together in one bed
    Hie diddle unkum tweedle.
The mouse at the foot; the man at the
head
    Hie diddle unkum tweedle.
    Oh, hie diddle unkum, harum tarum,
Thru the town of Ramsey.
    Hie diddle unkum, down to the sea,
    Hie diddle unkum tweedle.

They both went to church on Sunday,
    too
And they both sat together in one pew

One day the mouse took sick and died
And the tailor he sat down and cried

He cried so 'til he passed away
Now they're both together so the
    people say

So, if you hear a rustling round your
    house
Just think on the story of the tailor
    and mouse

Am

F
x

C
x

Em

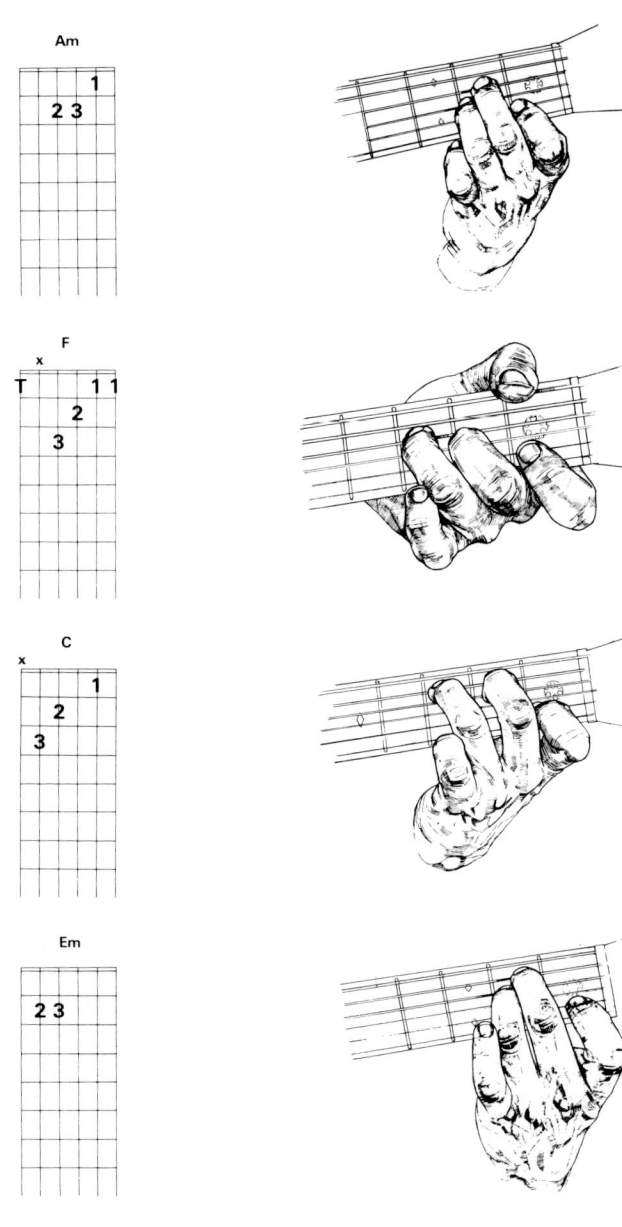

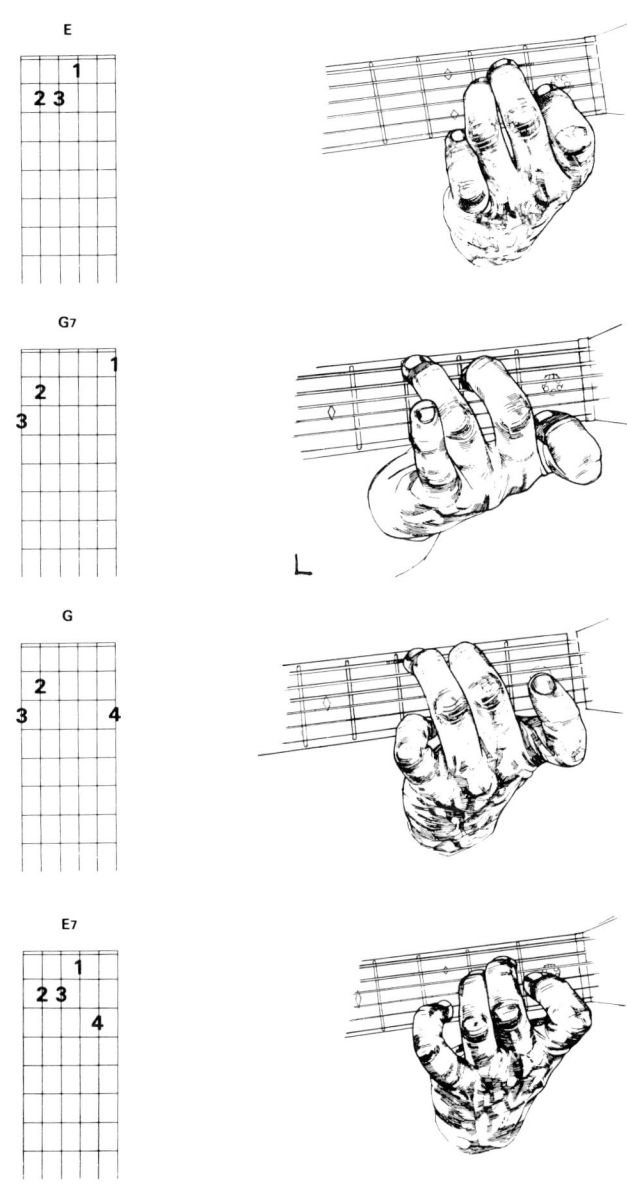

This is one of the very first songs that I learned as a child, so naturally, when I got my first guitar at the age of nine, it was a tune which I longed to play. However, my small hands couldn't hold down the chord of F. Try as I might, they just wouldn't stretch, and I couldn't get my thumb onto that sixth string. If you find the full chord of F too difficult to play at this stage, don't worry. Instead of playing thumb plucks on the sixth string, play them on the fourth string instead, like this:

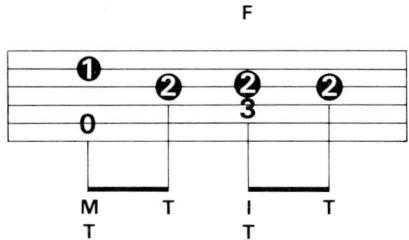

There are many ways of playing the chord of F—and every other chord, of course.

At the back of the book is a small "Chord Bank." When you have a spare moment or two sometime, why not dip into it and learn a new fingering?

Before you try the next song, I want to introduce you to some new tablature signs. They're the signs that we use to show a HAMMER-ON and a PULL-OFF.

What is meant by a hammer-on?

Well, let us suppose that you're playing a tune, and you want to play the open third string, followed by the third string held down behind the second fret. How would you do it? Well the obvious way would be to do just that: pluck the string open, then fret it behind the second fret and pluck it again. Right! But we do have, at least sometimes, yet another method—the hammer-on.

Here's how it's done:

Pluck the third string open. Then, while it's still ringing, bring your fretting finger hard down onto it, just behind the second fret, and you get a new note ringing out!

It looks like this:

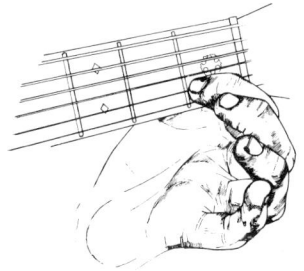 

Make sure that you allow the first note to ring out for its full time before you hammer-on to produce the second note. It should sound:

DUR! RUM! *not* DURRUM.

This is shown on the tablature by linking the two notes concerned with a bracket and marking an H above.

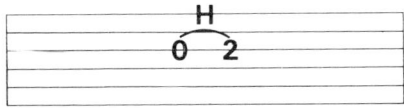

The opposite of a hammer-on is called a pull-off.

Here is how you play it:

Pluck the fretted string. Then, while the note is still ringing out, you pull slightly to one side with the finger which is holding the string down; now let the string slip out from underneath—and there rings your second note.

It looks like this:

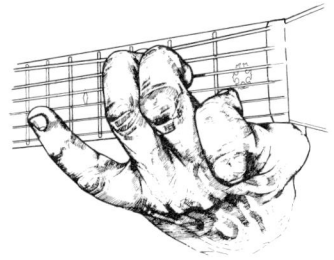 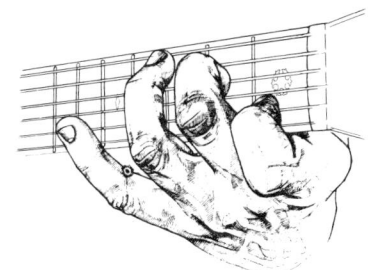

On tablature, we show it thus:

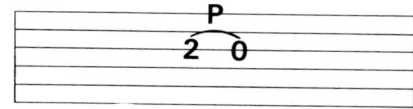

Simple as they are, both of these "tricks" may take a little time to master.

Don't give up. They're worth every drop of sweat.

By the way, in both the hammer-on and the pull-off don't forget to allow the first notes to ring out fully before you move the finger.

Remember the sound:

      DUR! RUM!   *not*   DURRUM

OK?

Let's move on to the next song, which uses both techniques.

"THE ROVING GAMBLER"

Arr. Pearse

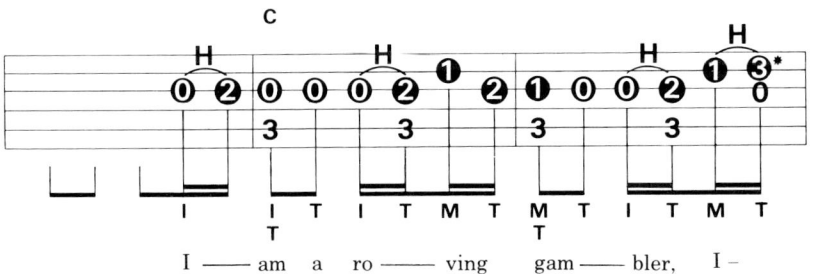

I —— am a ro —— ving gam —— bler, I –

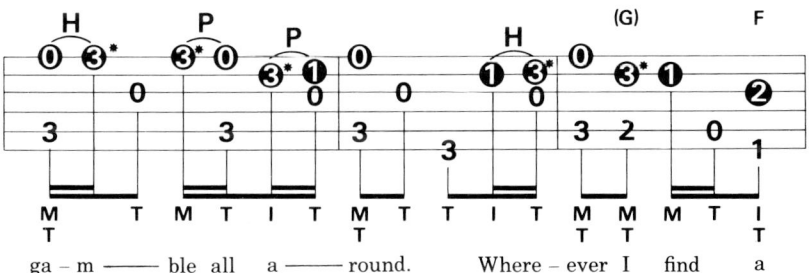

ga – m —— ble all a —— round. Where – ever I find a

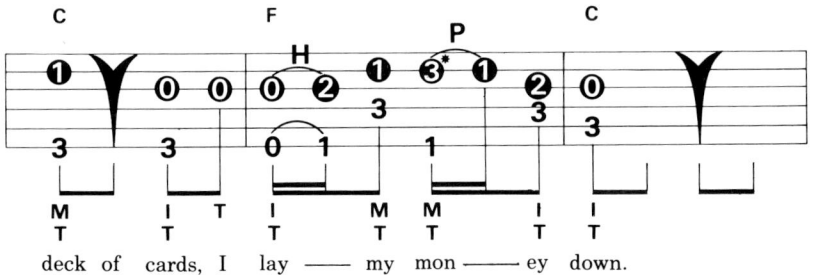

deck of cards, I lay —— my mon —— ey down.

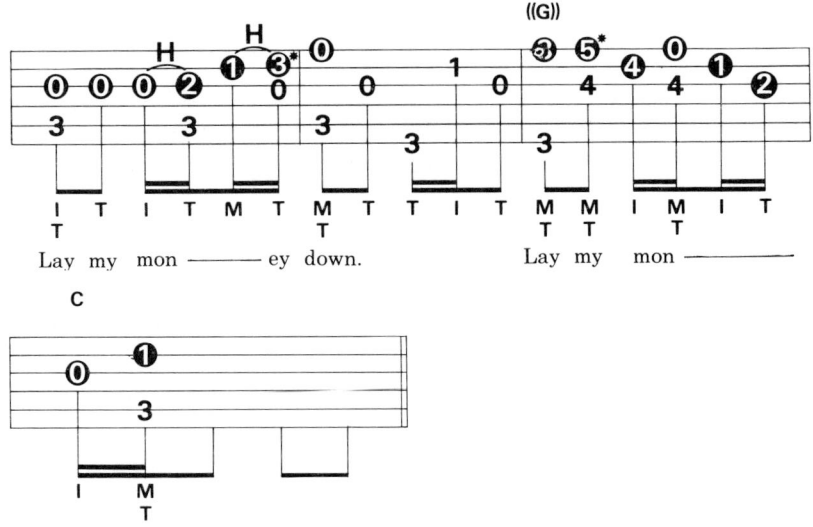

Lay my mon ———— ey down.   Lay my mon ————

— ey down.

I had not been in Sugarland
Many more weeks than three,
When I met up with this pretty little girl
And she fell in love with me.
    Fell in love with me.
    Fell in love with me.

She wore her hair on the top of her head
In that fancy Charleston way,
And she did most ev'rything she could
To try to make me stay.

But I've gambled out in 'Frisco,
Gambled up in Maine,
I'm headed down to Georgia
To gamble my last game.

I am a roving gambler,
I gamble all around.
Wherever I find a deck of cards
I lay my money down.

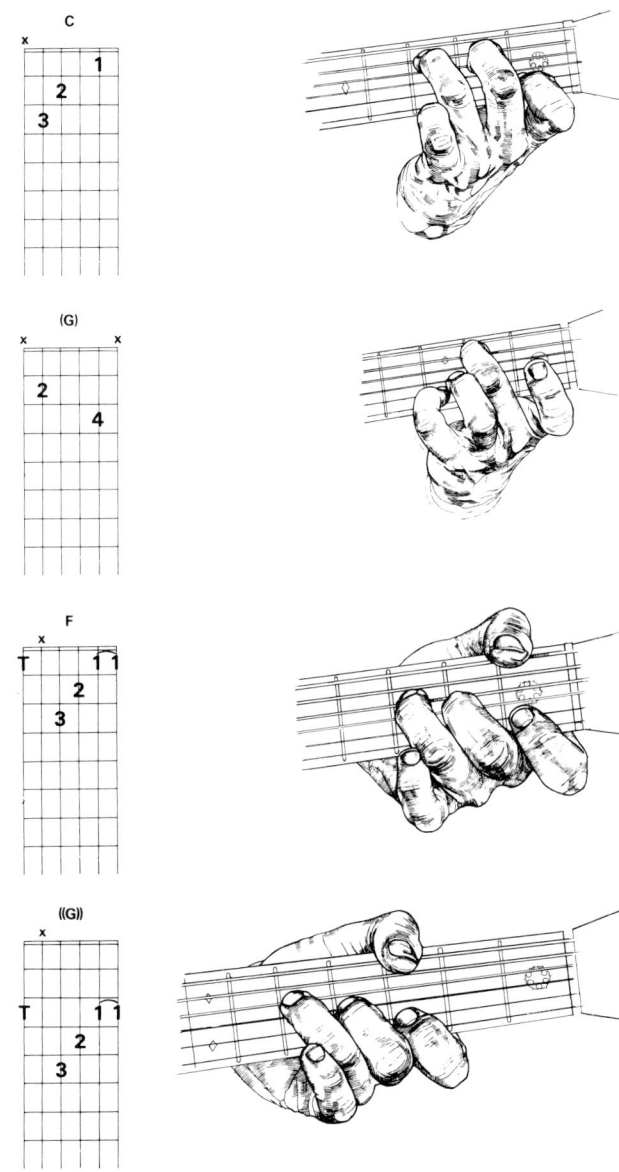

How was it?

Many people find that the awkward thing with both the hammer-on and the pull-off is that it's sometimes difficult for them to synchronize the second notes if they happen to fall on the same beat as a thumb count. For instance, take a look at the start of BAR FOUR:

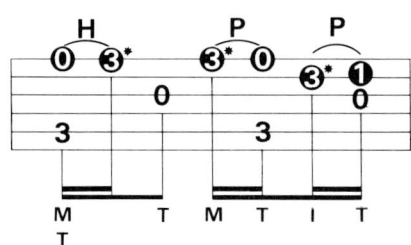

Here the first note falls on count ONE, a thumb count, the actual hammer-on falling on an "AND" count. Not too difficult to play, but let's move along the bar to counts THREE and FOUR. Here the rhythm AND-THREE AND-FOUR is provided by two pull-off notes.

Here is the best way to practice the bar:

Hold down a C chord.

Count ONE	Thumb plucks the fifth string held down behind the third fret, while *simultaneously* the middle finger plucks the first string open.
"AND" count	The fourth finger (remember * ?) hammers down on the first string just behind the third fret.
Count TWO	Thumb plucks the open third string.
"AND" count	Middle finger plucks the first string held down behind the third fret, by the fourth finger of the left hand.
Count THREE	Thumb plucks the fifth string held down behind the third fret, while *simultaneously* the fourth finger pulls-off from the third fret on the first string.

"AND" count	Index finger plucks the second string held down behind the third fret, by the fourth finger of the left hand.
Count FOUR	Thumb plucks the open third string, while *simultaneously* the fourth finger pulls-off from the third fret on the second string, allowing it to ring at its normal fret position, the first.

Now let's take a look at BARS SIX and TWELVE:

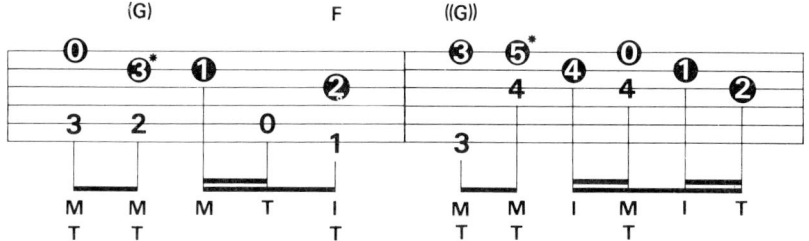

Quite often we use more than one way of playing a chord in a tune. In this one, for example, we use three different fingerings for the chord of G. To make it easier to locate the fingering that you need in the chords which I've set out with each tune, you will often see a bracket or brackets enclosing some of the chords in the arrangement. When you come across this, just look for a similarly marked chord "Diagram and Picture" group. By the way, be on your guard for the simultaneous bass and melody hammers-on in BAR EIGHT:

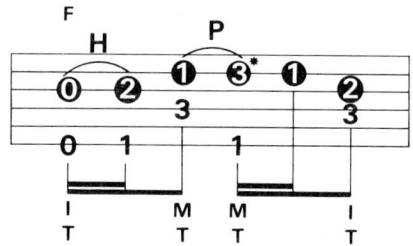

"IN GOOD KING ARTHUR'S DAY"

Arr. Pearse

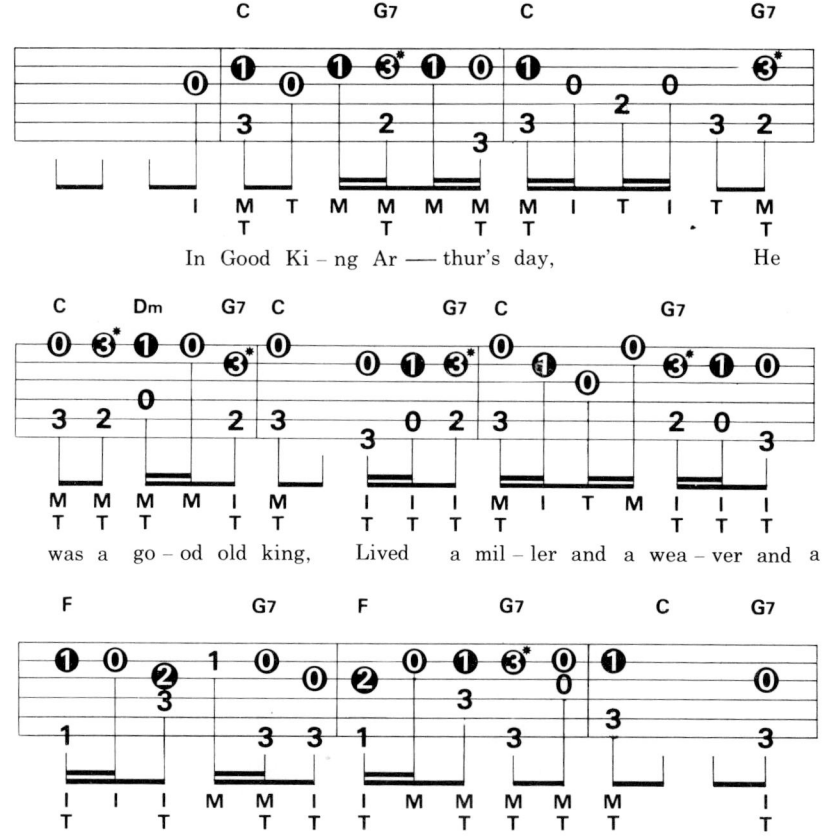

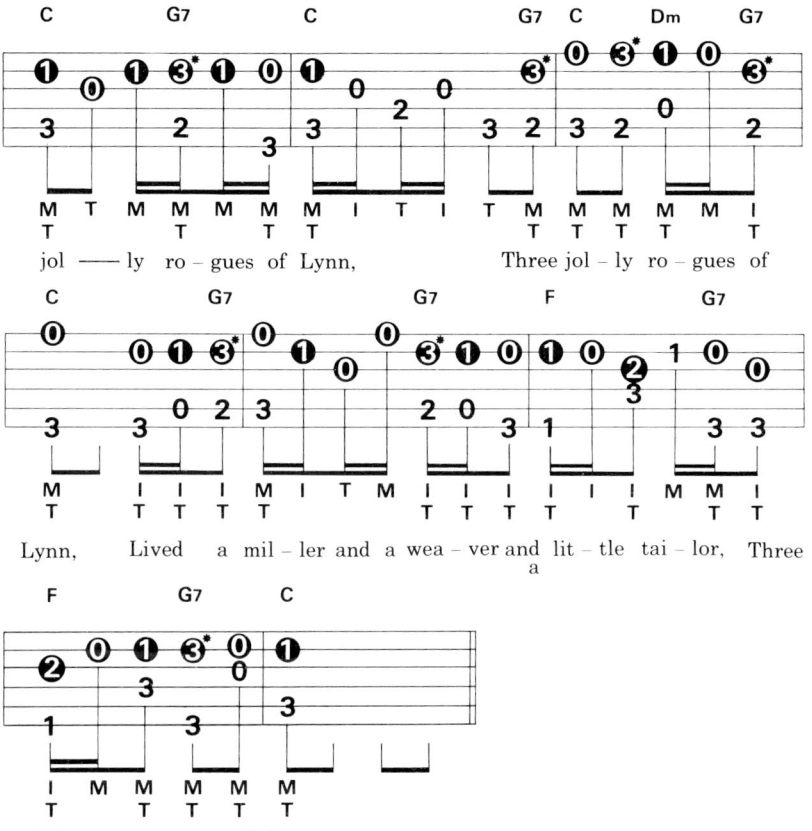

Now, the miller he stole some grain,
And the weaver he stole some yarn,
And the little tailor he stole broadcloth
To keep those three rogues warm.

The miller was drowned in his dam,
And the weaver was hanged in his yarn,
And the Devil put his eye on the
 tailor boy
With the broadcloth under his arm.

The miller still swims in his dam,
And the weaver still swings in his
 yarn,
But the little tailor boy goes
 skipping thru Hell
With the broadcloth under his arm.

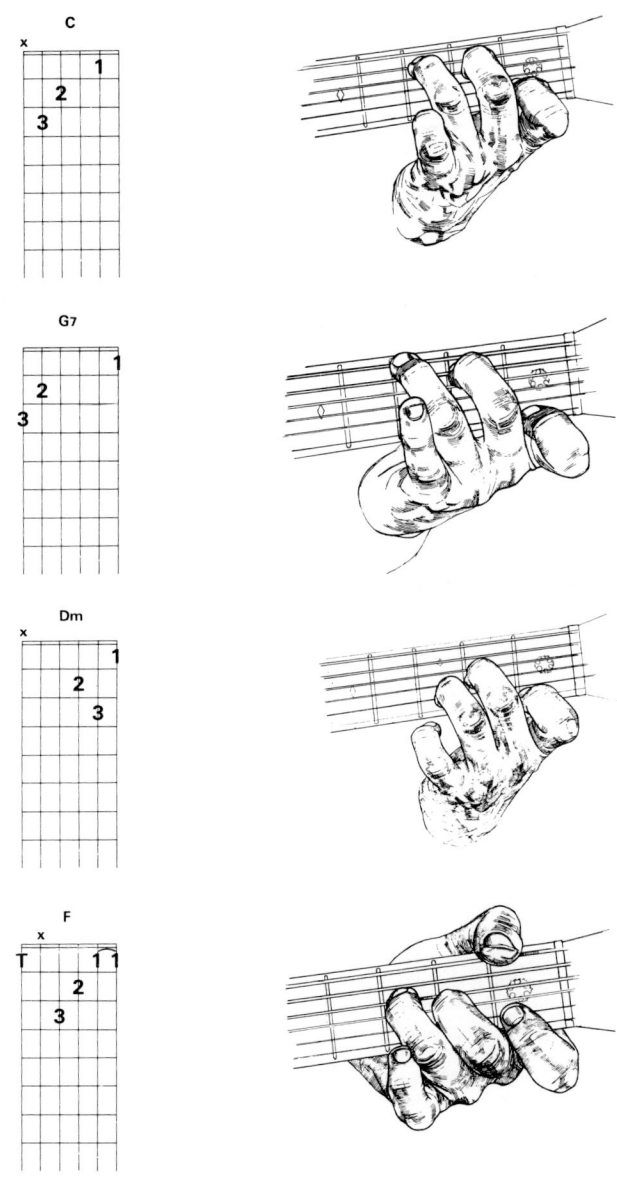

C

G7

Dm

F

This is another of my favorite tunes, as it lends itself to the addition of some very effective counterpoint and TEXTURING.

Texturing is a term that we sometimes use to describe the way that the emphases of a tune vary slightly from bar to bar. Look at BAR FIVE, for example:

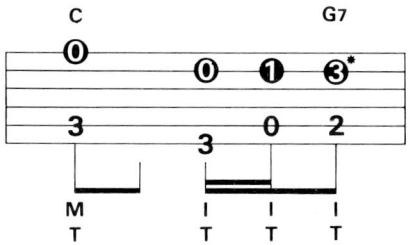

The rhythm is: ONE ... THREE-AND FOUR.

Normally the thumb would not play on an "AND" count (except maybe when alternating with the first finger in a fast single-string run). However, the use of it in this case makes possible a counterpoint line which stretches to link up with the first count of the next bar.

"THE DYING COWBOY"

Arr. Pearse

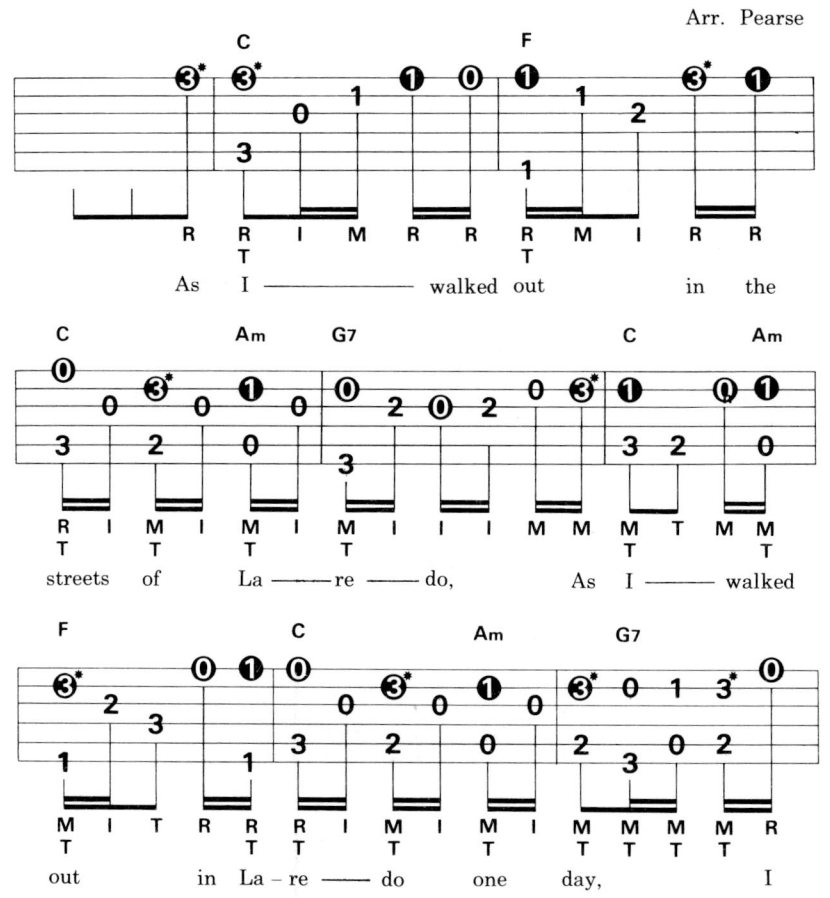

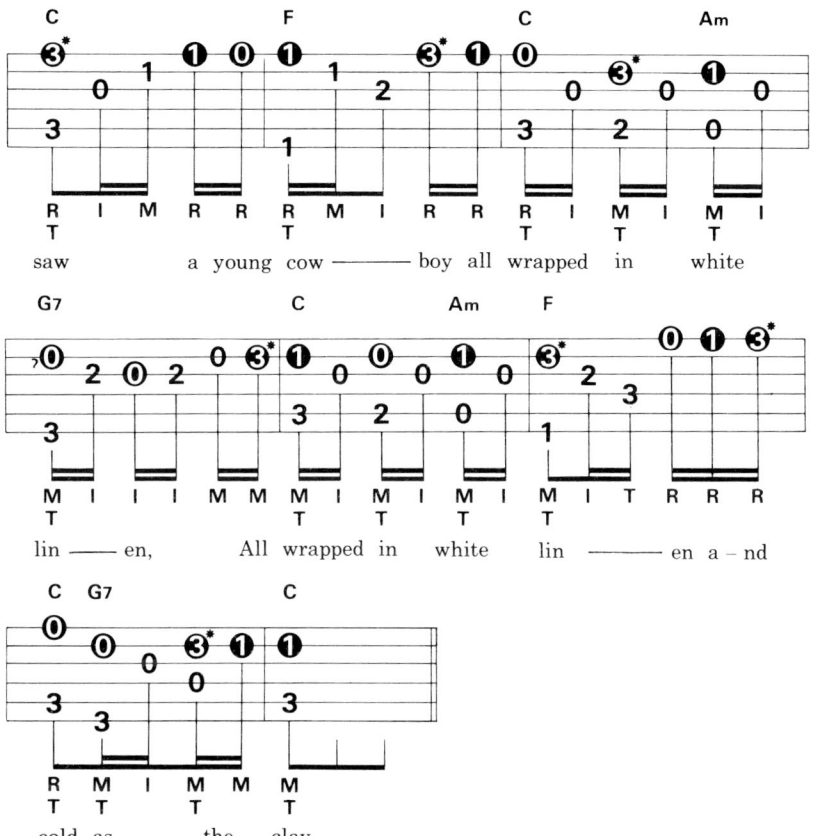

As I walked out in the streets of Laredo,
As I walked out in Laredo one day,
I saw a young cowboy all wrapped in white linen,
All wrapped in white linen and cold as the clay.

"I see by your outfit that you are a cowboy,"
These words he did say as I made to pass by.
"Come sit down beside me and hear my sad story.
I'm shot in the breast and I surely must die."

"It was once in the saddle I used to go dashing,
Once in the saddle I used to go gay.

(continued)

It was first to the card house and then to the cat house,
Now I'm shot in the breast and I'm dying today."

"So get sixteen gamblers to carry my coffin,
Six pretty women to sing me a song.
Take me down to Long Valley and lay the sod over me,
For I am a young cowboy and I know I've done wrong."

"So it's beat the drum slowly, but it's play the fife merrily,
And it's play me a jig not some old mournful song.
And it's cover my coffin with bunches of roses,
And give them to the ladies as you carry me on."

(Repeat first verse)

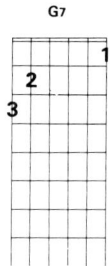

This three-four (waltz-time) song must surely be one of the most widely traveled folk songs in the world. It's known in Ireland, England, Australia, all through the States, and versions go by many, many names: "The Unfortunate Rake," "The Irish Lass," "The Royal Albion," "Beat the Drum Slowly," "Streets of Laredo," "The Dying Stockman," "Wrap Me Up in My Tarpaulin Jacket," "St. James Infirmary" and so on.

As this is your first meeting with a tune in three-four tablature, let's work out the rhythm of a few bars together.

Look at BAR TWO, for instance:

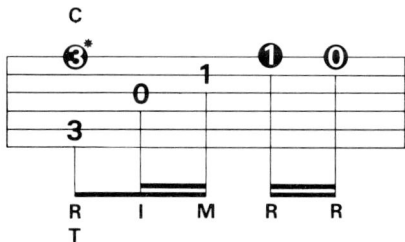

This is another example of a tune where some of the basic counts are played by a finger rather than a thumb pluck.

The rhythm here is: ONE AND-TWO AND-THREE.

While in BAR FIFTEEN,

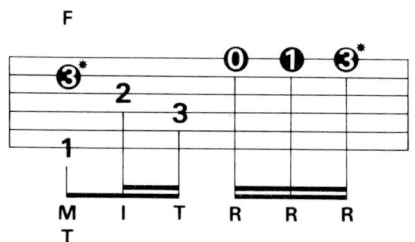

the rhythm would be: ONE AND-TWO AND-THREE-AND.
Not so difficult is it?
In BAR FOUR,

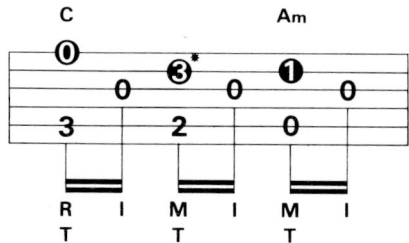

the rhythm is: ONE-AND TWO-AND THREE-AND.

So it is in BAR THIRTEEN, although the thumb plucks only once, the remainder of the bar being taken up by a run played by the index and middle fingers.

Again, in this tune I have tried to include interesting textures and counterpoint; but as I said earlier, don't be afraid to experiment for yourself.

BEFORE YOU TRY THE NEXT SONG : THE SLIDE

From time to time we fret a string one fret or more below or above the note that we actually want to hear, then while it's still ringing, we slide our fretting finger to the correct fret. This is called, naturally enough, a SLIDE.

On tablature we show it like this:

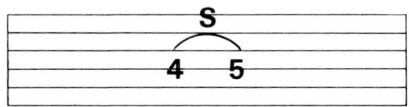

At home I have a basset hound called Hercules and he has a very definite personality, especially when he's being taken out for a walk. He just sets his own pace, and everyone else has to fit in. You can set your own pace, too, in this next tune.

"WALKING THE BASSET"

Comp. Pearse

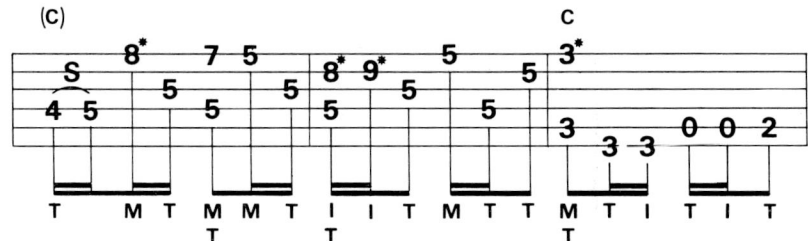

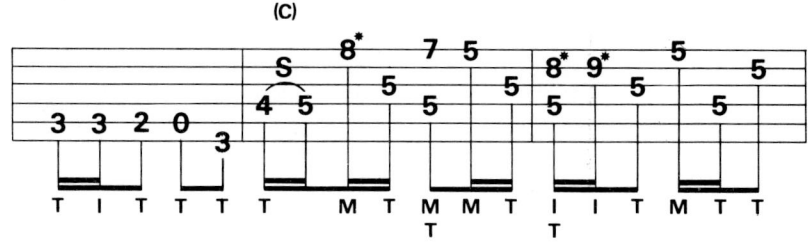

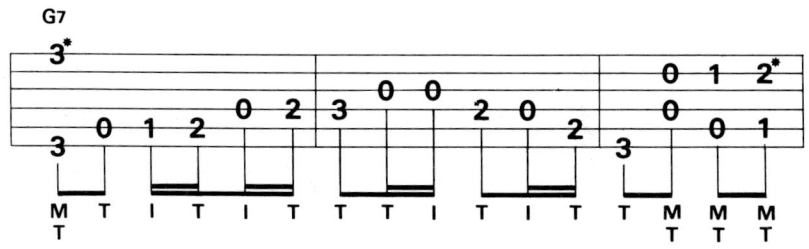

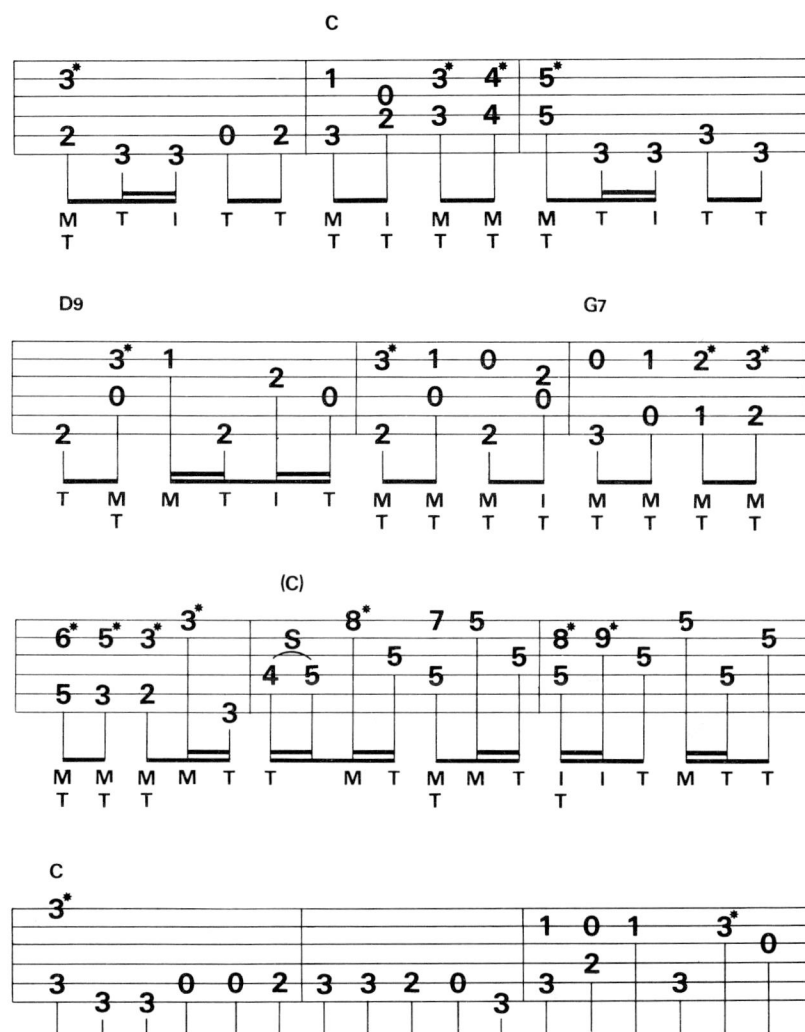

174

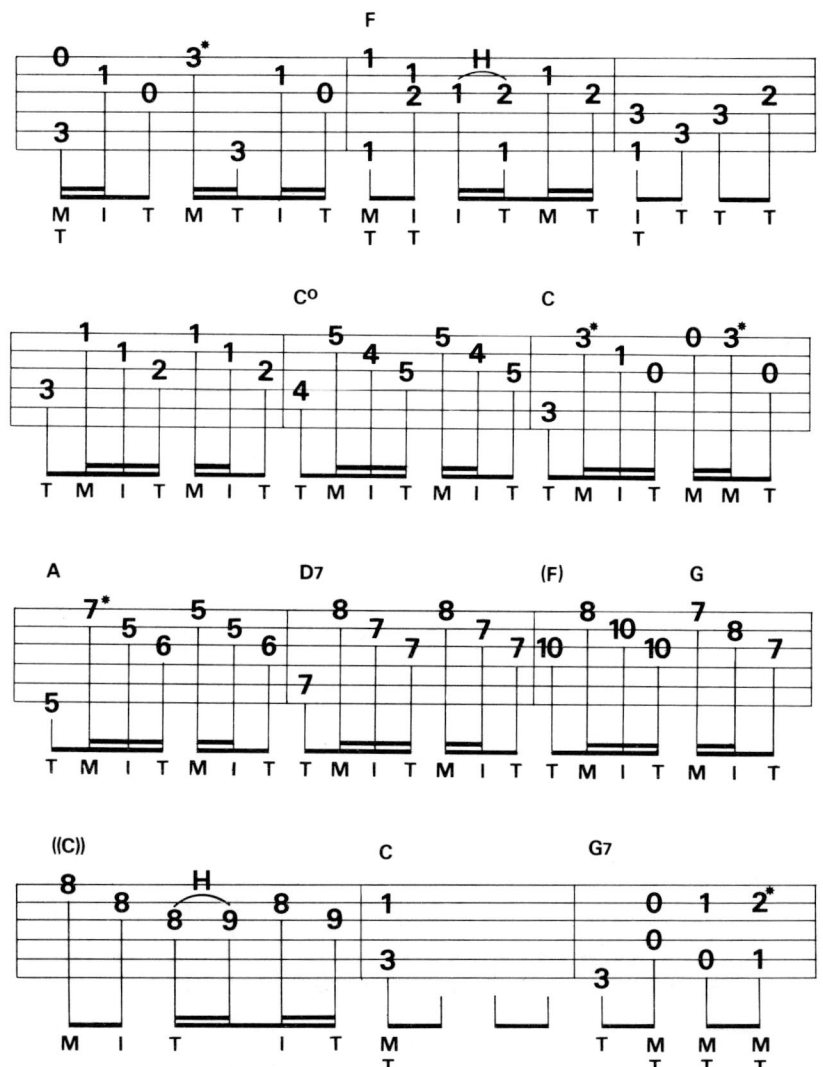

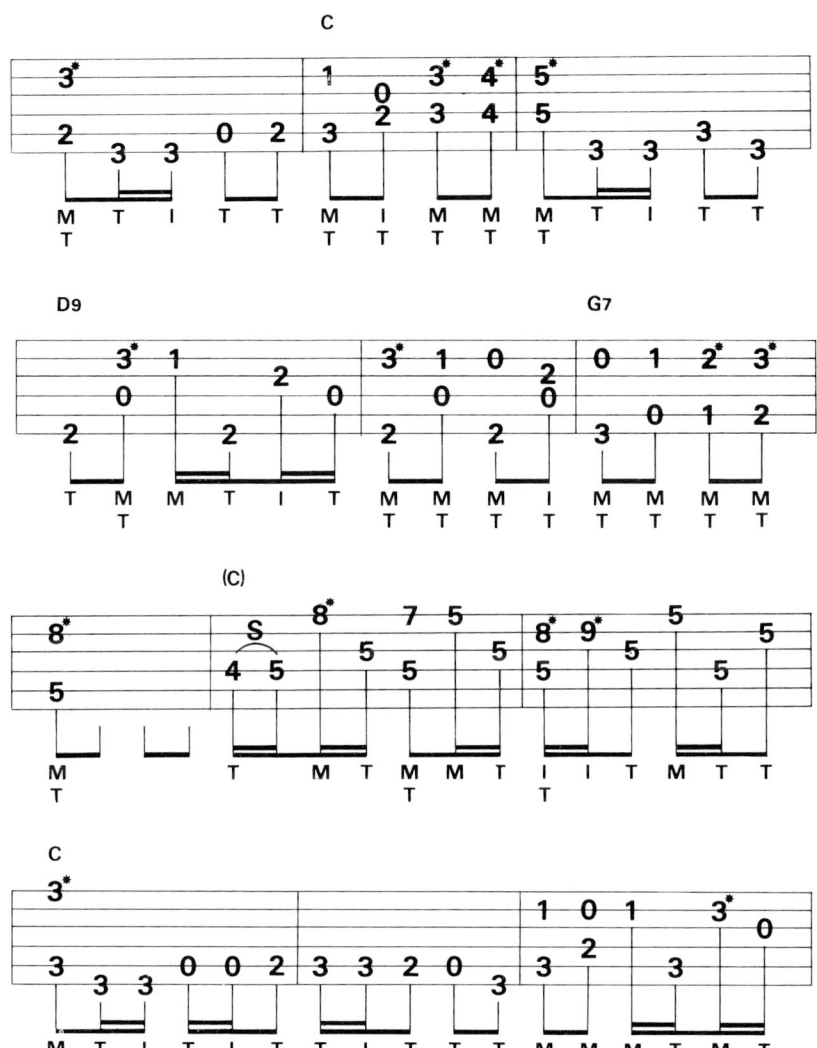

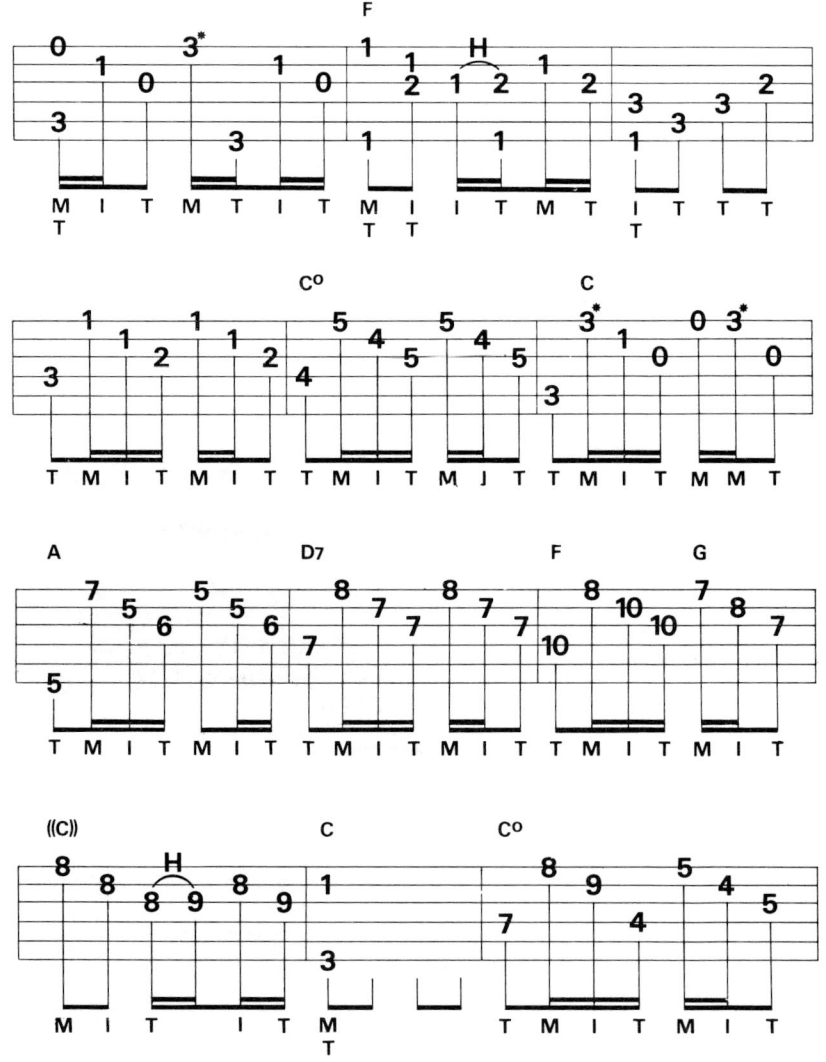

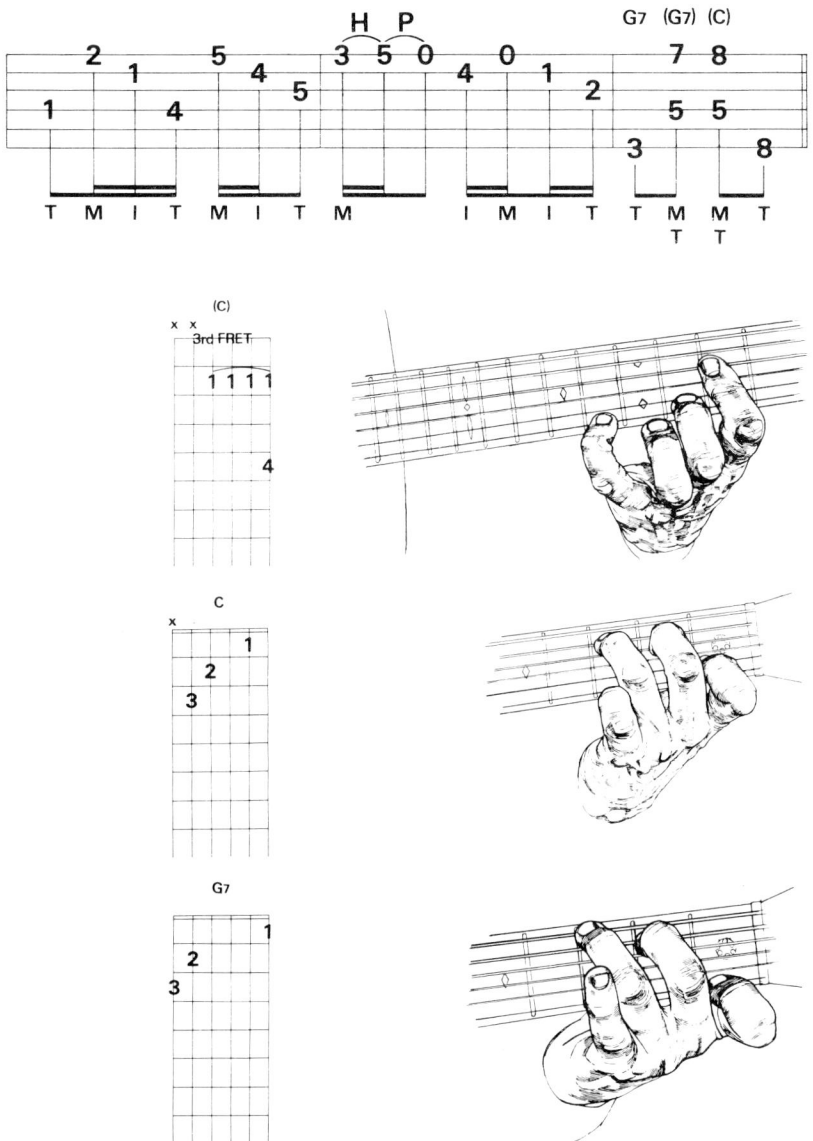

D9

F

(C°)

A

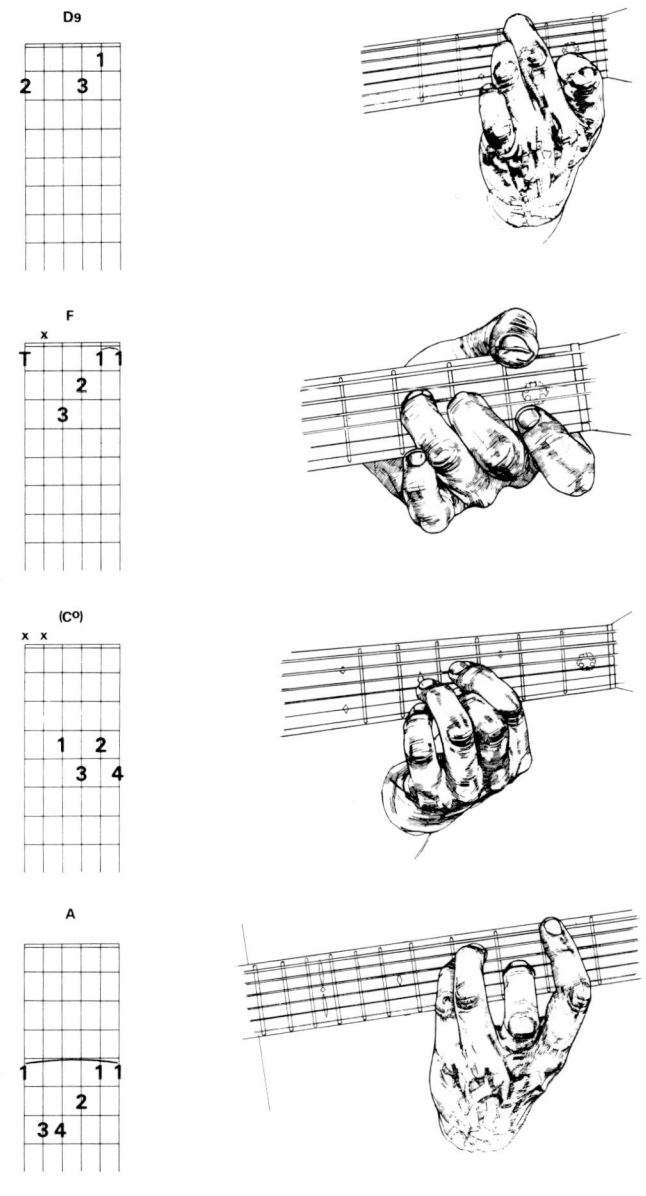

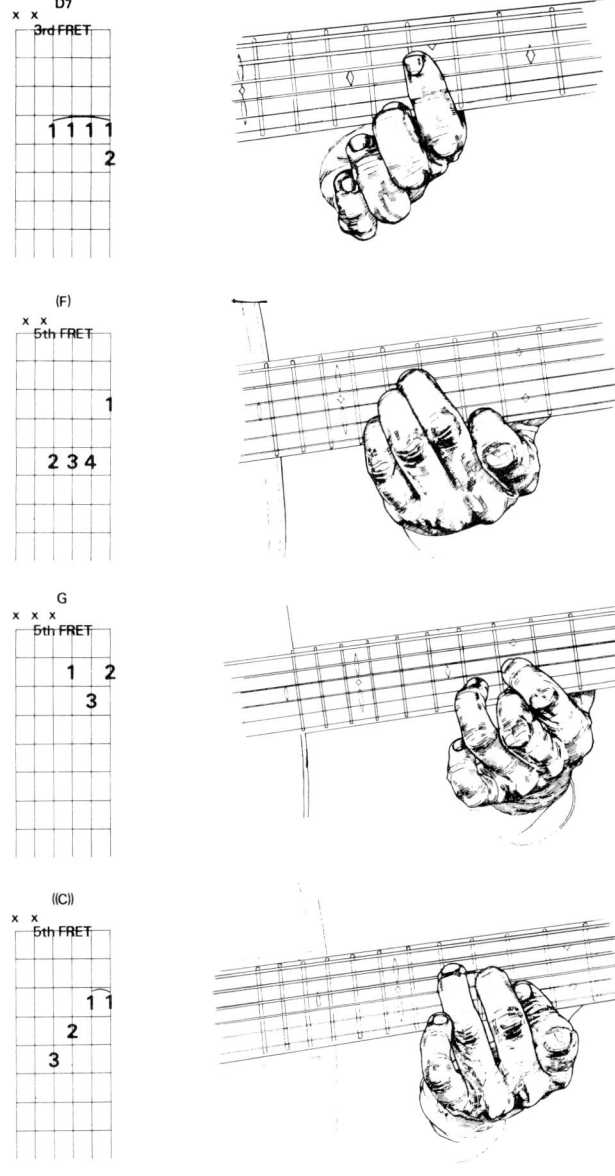

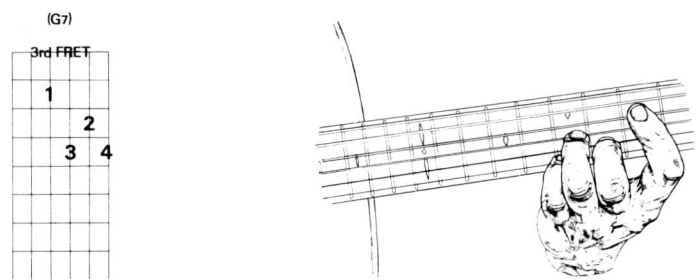

I'll wager that you came a bit unstuck in BAR TWENTY-FIVE.

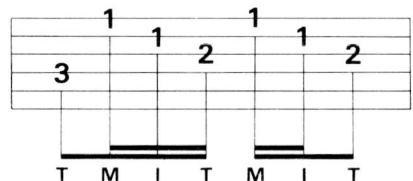

The rhythm is not easy. "Walking the Basset" is a ragtime guitar solo, and like most guitar rags, it is heavily influenced by the piano rag music of the '20s taking to itself many of the "riffs" and "tricks" developed by the old piano players. One of the most typical of these effects is the ROLL, the rhythm of which is:

ONE AND-TWO-AND THREE-AND FOUR.

If you take a look at the bar, and compare it with BARS TWENTY-SIX to THIRTY, all of which contain rolls,

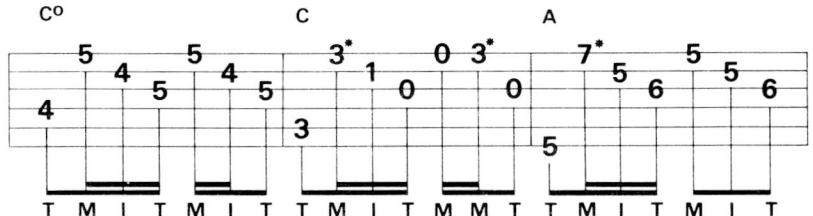

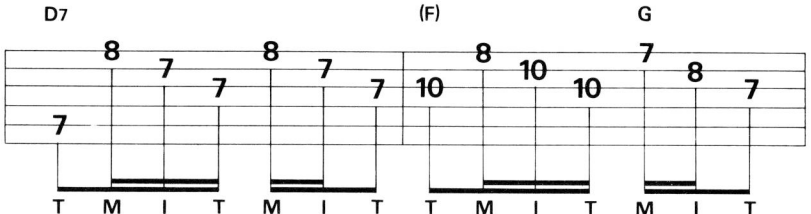

you'll see that the notes make a quite definite and easily recognizable shape, rather like this:

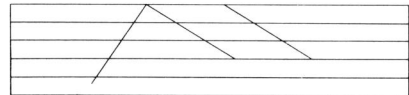

Try to memorize this shape. You'll come across it many times in your playing.

"SHERMAN SHAMBLEFINGERS"

Comp. Pearse

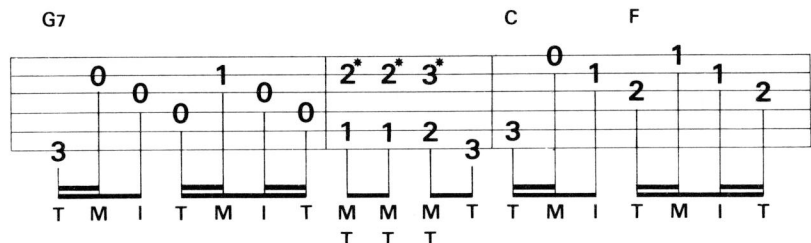

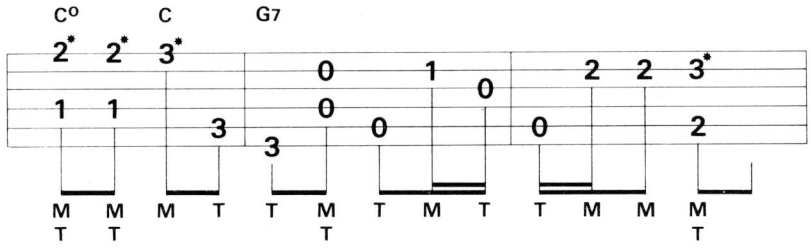

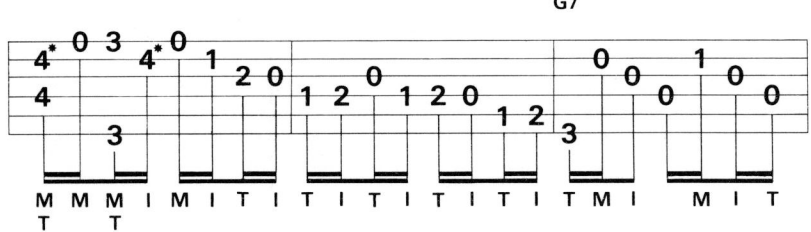

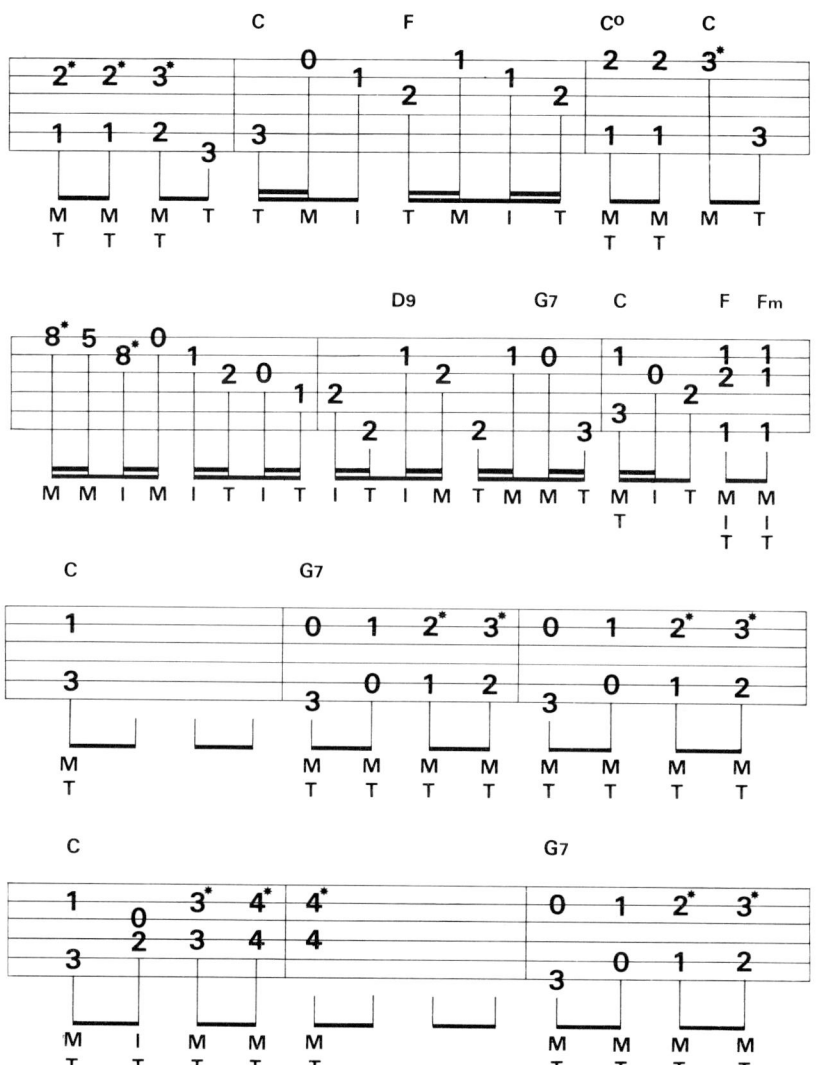

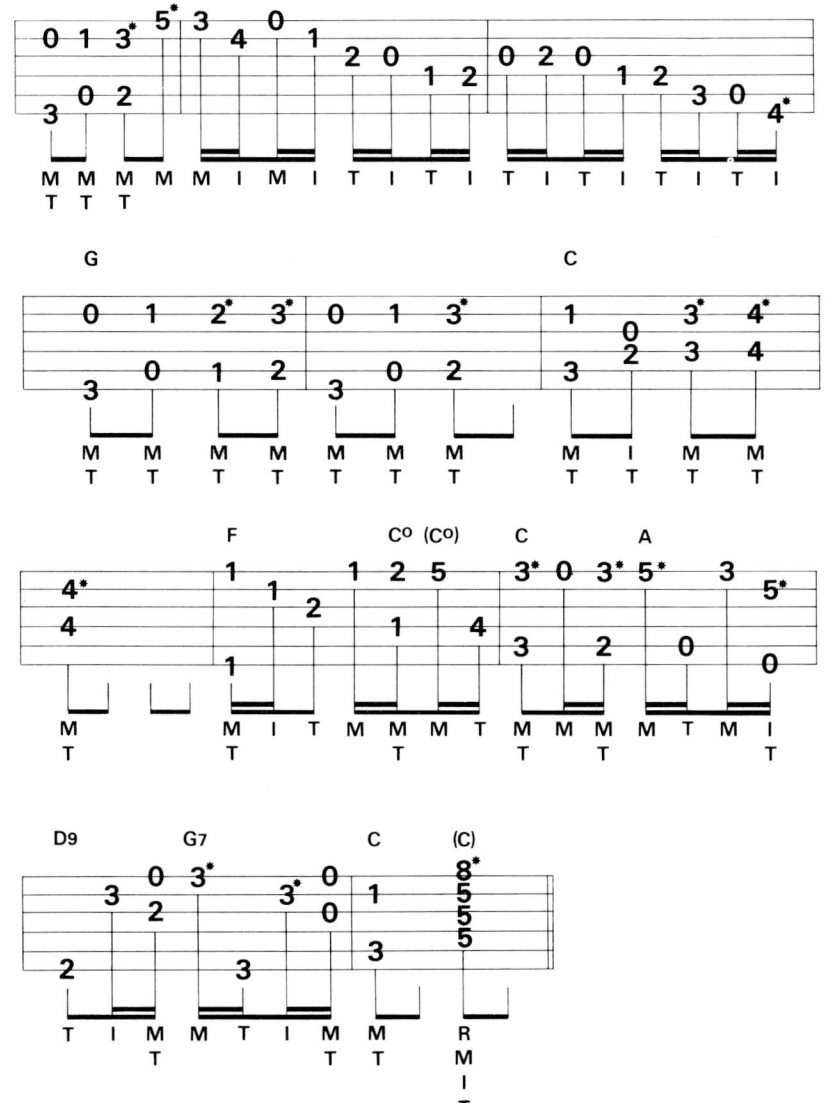

184

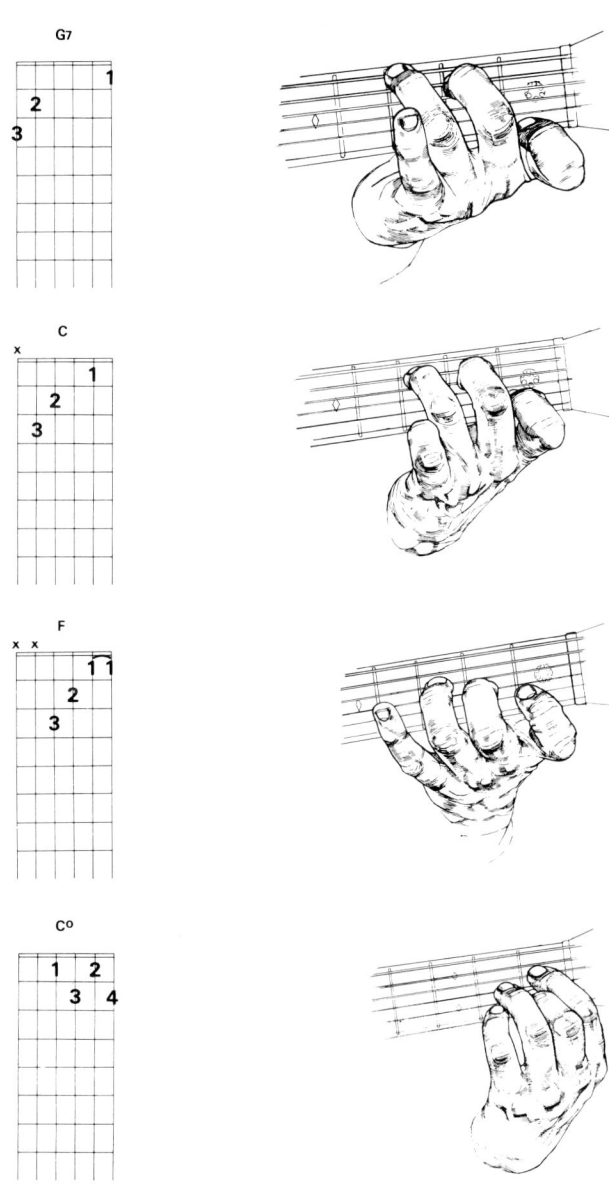

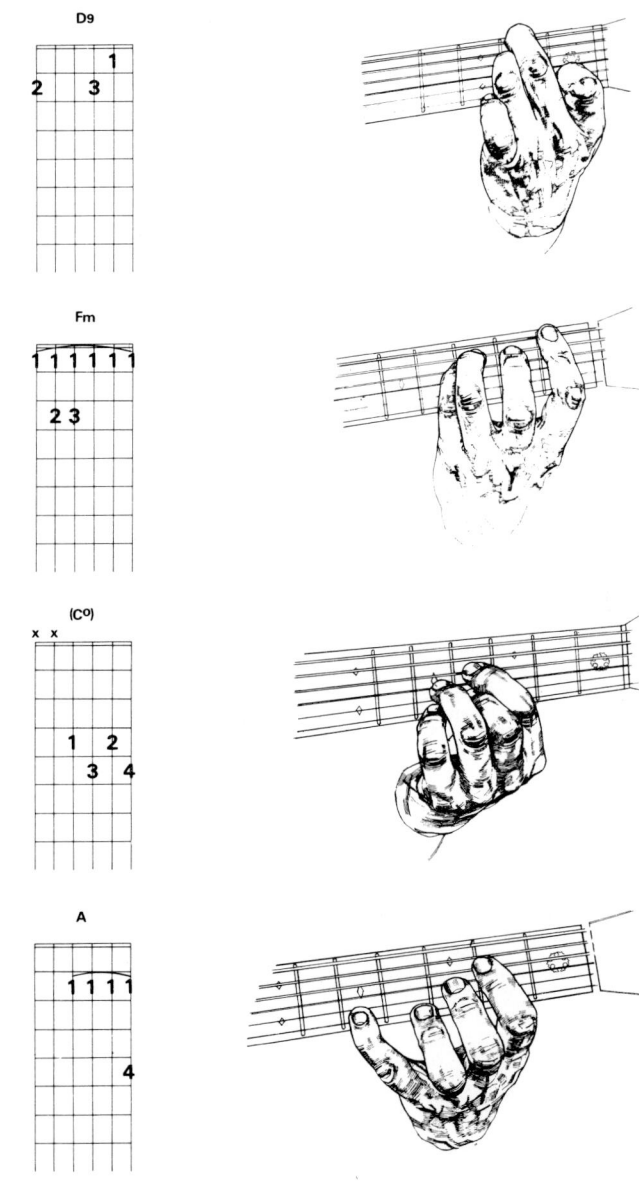

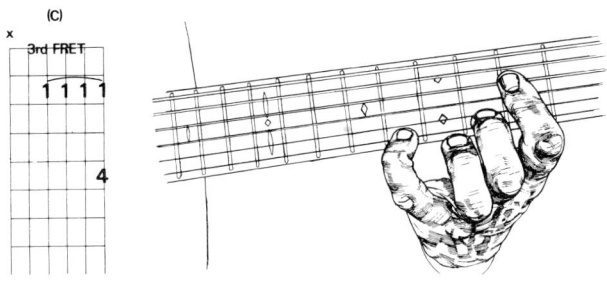

BAR ONE

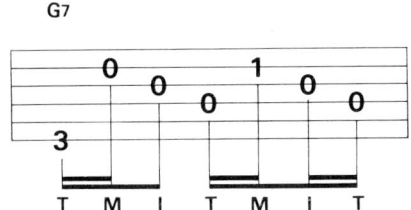

is a typical roll (did you recognize it?), but the rhythm emphases are different from those which you met in "Walking the Basset."

How did you get on in BARS SEVEN and EIGHT?

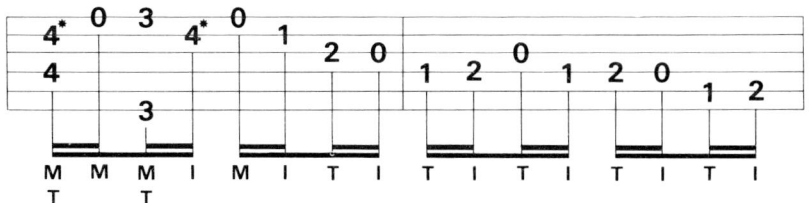

They contain a riff—or stock phrase—which again derives wholly from the '20s piano style. Practice it until it sounds as fluid as your roll.

By the way, the rhythm is: ONE-AND TWO-AND THREE-AND FOUR-AND —but I'm sure you'd already worked it out for yourself!

"O DANNY BOY"

Arr. Pearse

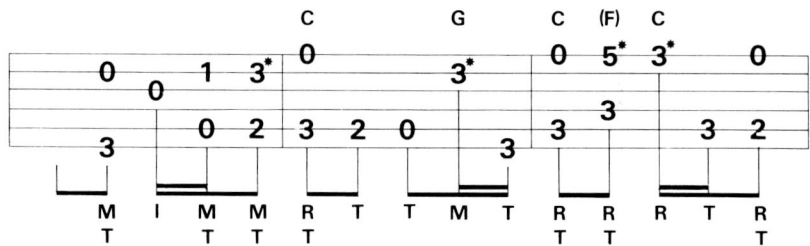

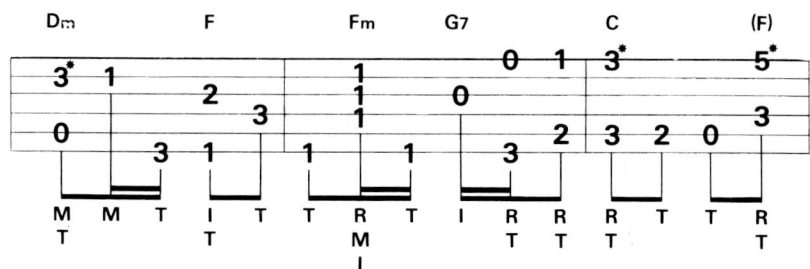

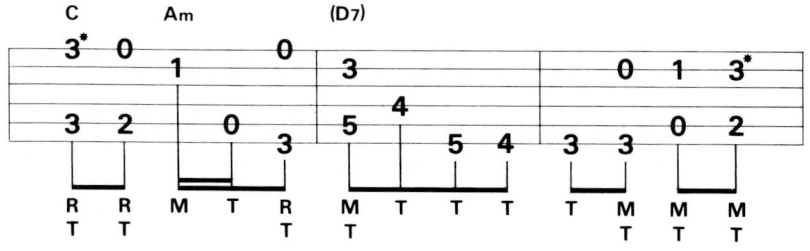

189

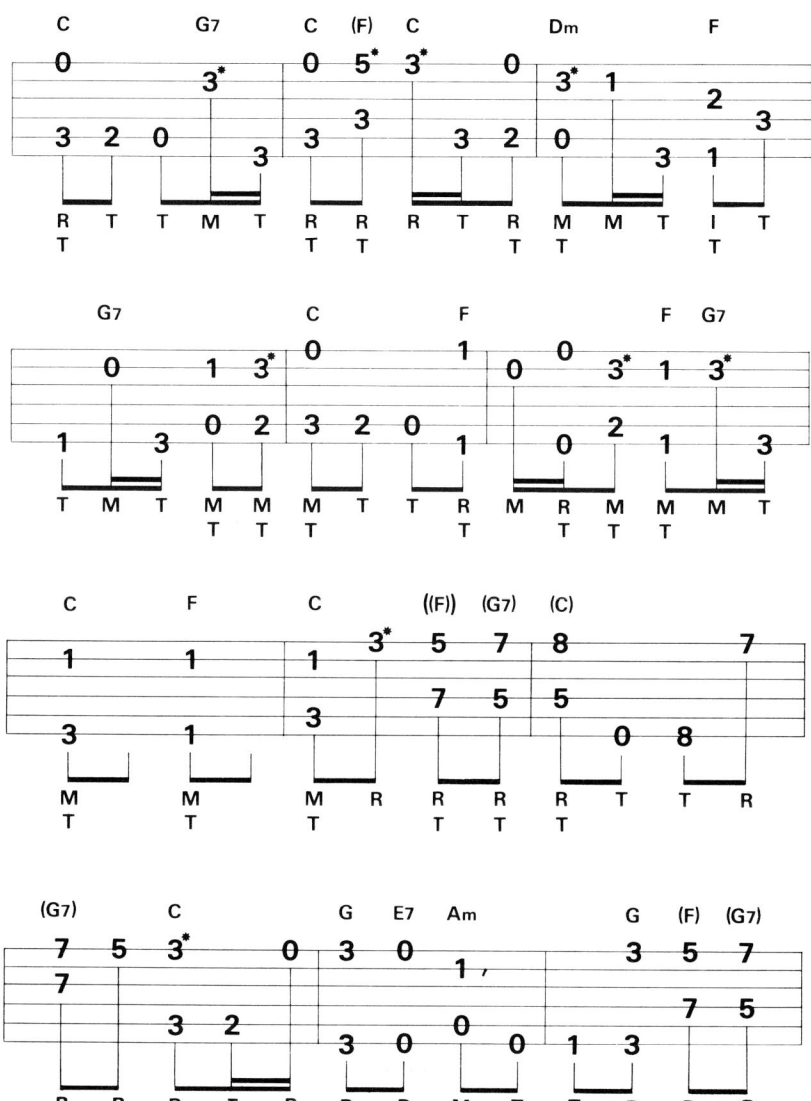

190

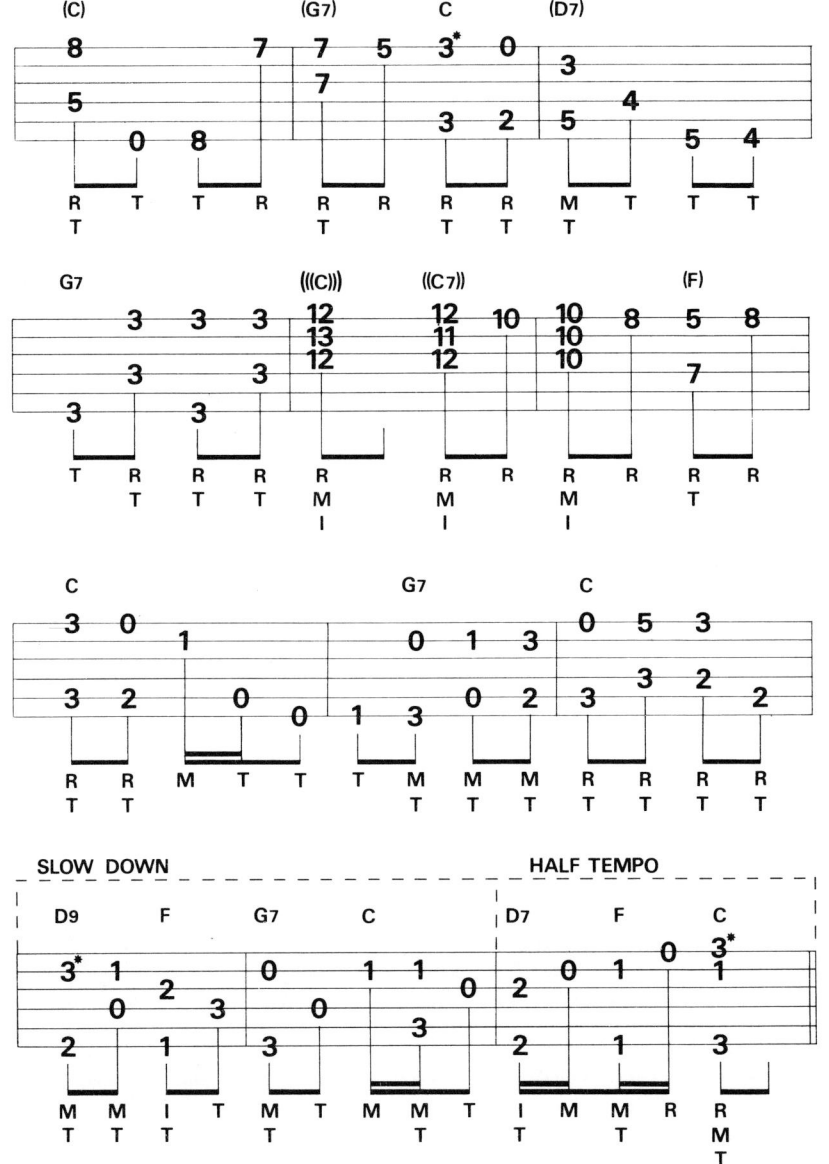

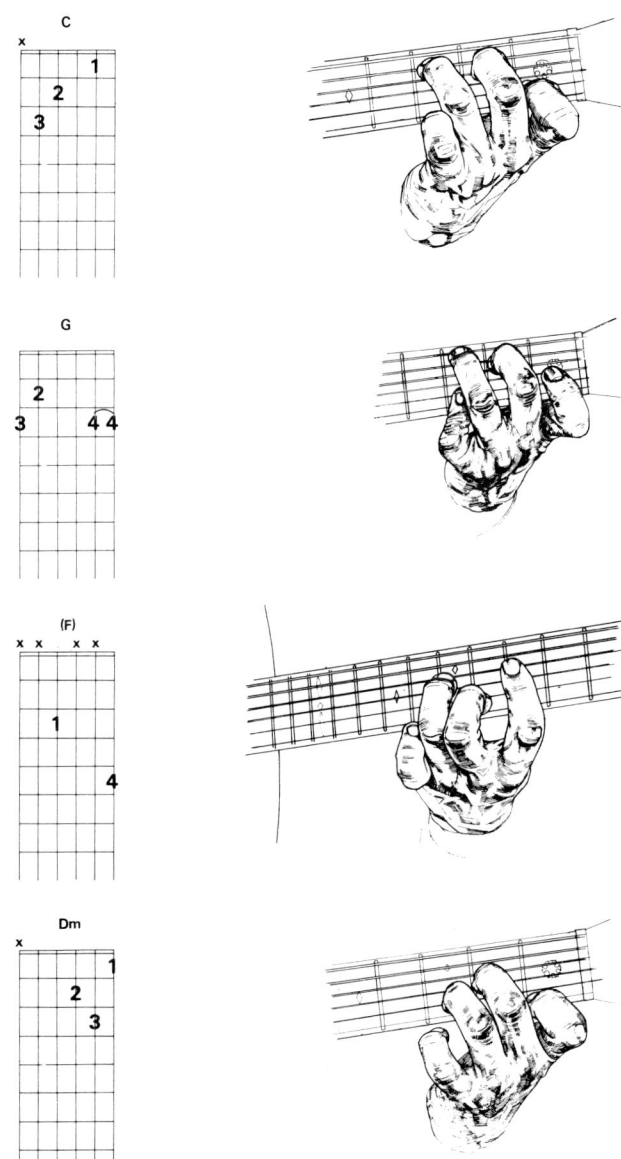

F

Fm

G7

Am

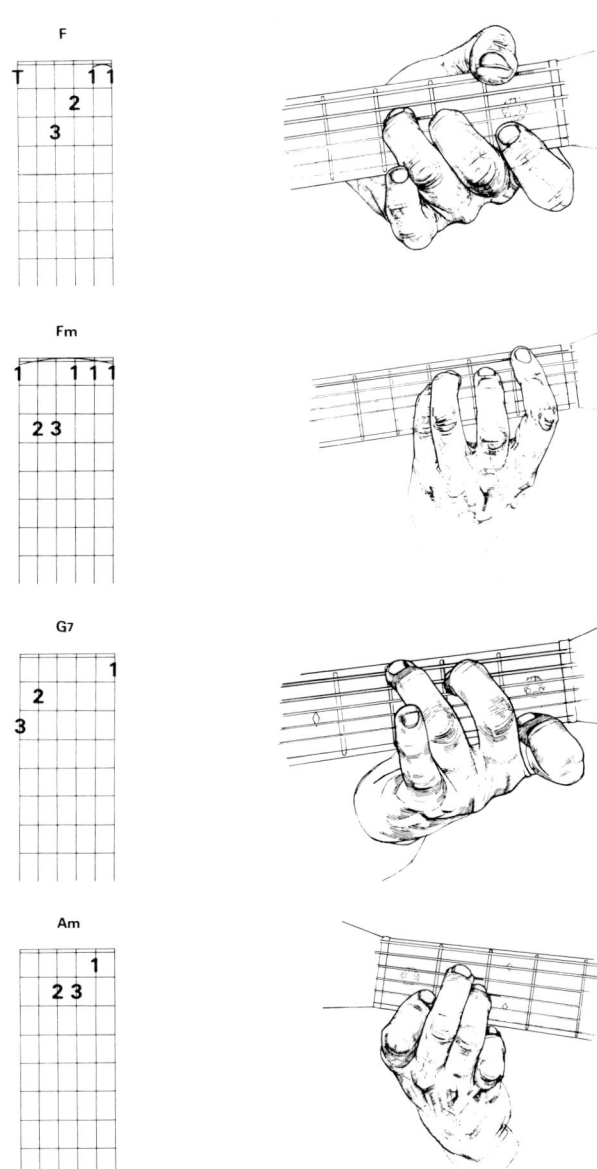

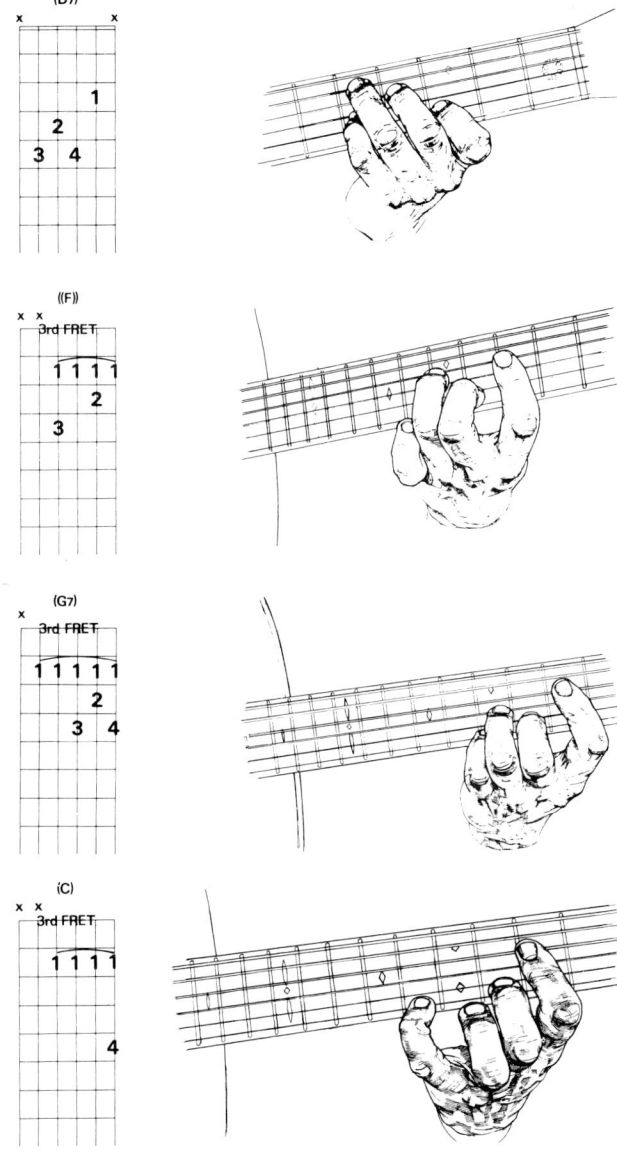

194

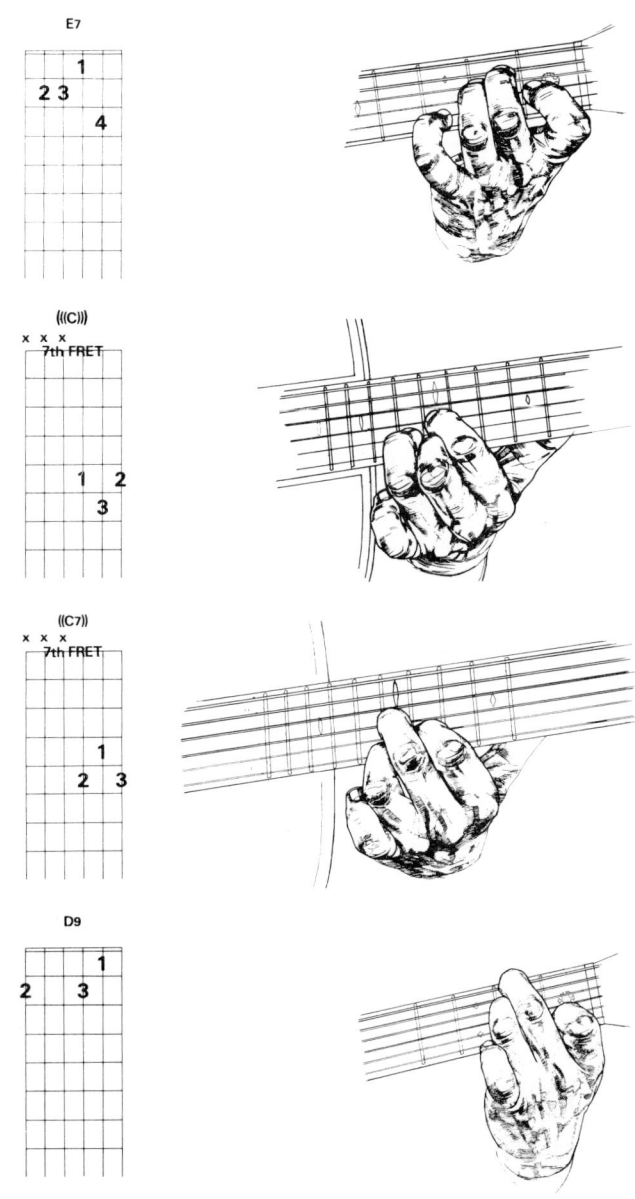

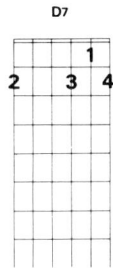

This arrangement uses a fairly jazz-oriented approach to the playing, with the thumb laying down a bass-fiddle line throughout, against a cleanly picked (hopefully!), finger-played melody. Because the thumb is playing a line rather than a rock, I would suggest that you place your right-hand fingers in this position:

— first finger on the third string

— second finger on the second string

— third finger on the first string

Although the arrangement is quite complex in places, there is nothing that should cause you any real worry. As always, however, check each bar through before you attempt it, and as there are so many chord changes and unusual fingerings, check which particular fingerings you will need before you start playing a bar. The only rhythm query that you might have concerns BAR ONE:

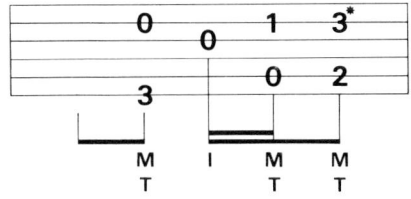

Here the rhythm is:

. . .   TWO AND-THREE   FOUR

When you've mastered the tune, experiment by adding the occasional extra string into the arrangement. It doesn't always work, but to give you some ideas, here is the first line with some suggested additions:

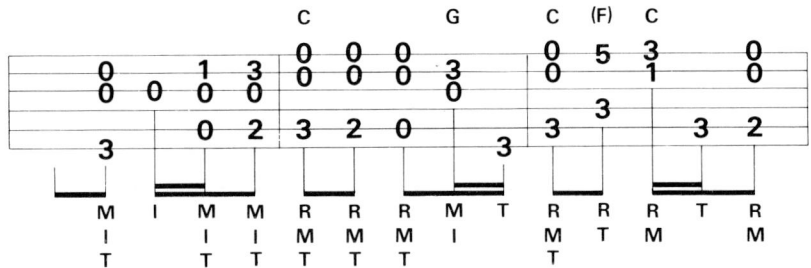

And so to the last tune in the book — a tune, moreover, in an OPEN TUNING that we call G TUNING. An open tuning just means that the unfretted strings of your guitar in this tuning will produce a chord. In this case, the chord of G.

Take a look at our old friend, the halftone diagram, again:

A	B♭	B	C	C♯	D	E♭	E	F	F♯	G	A♭

Here is our normal tuning: E A D G B E.

And here are the notes of our new tuning: D G D G B D.

As you can see, the second, third and fourth string are unchanged; we only alter the first, fifth and sixth string pitches. We shall do this by using a mixture of halftone counting and ear training.

Here goes.

The easiest way to drop the first string to D is obviously to find the same D note on another string and match them. We'll use the second string.

How many steps are there between B and E? C, C♯, D, E♭ and E. Five!

Hold down the second string behind the fifth fret and pluck it. It should sound the same as the open first string. Now we want to drop the first down to D, so how many halftones lower is that? Two! So move your finger down two frets on the second string, down to the third; pluck it, then lower the first string down to this note. OK?

Now for the ear training. By this time your ear should be reasonably dependable, so this is a little test to see how accurate you can be. We now have our first string tuned to D. If you look at the notes of the new tuning, you'll see that we have two other D notes, on the fourth and sixth strings. We have the fourth string D already in tune (same as our standard tuning), so what I want you to do is to pluck your first string D, then your fourth string D, and then pluck your sixth string and lower it down by ear alone, to low D. With the other two D notes to help you, it shouldn't be too hard, but take it very slowly and see how you get on.

How was it?

OK?

Don't worry if you find it rather difficult at first, or even if you can't do it.

If you do find it impossible, you can always use the half-tone diagram and tune the sixth string that way.

Now for the fifth string. At present it is tuned to A, and we want it down to G. Well, if you tuned the last string by ear, why not have a go with this one? Our third string is a G, too, so just pluck it and drop the fifth string down. Again, you can rely on the halftone diagram if you get stuck.

Tune Guitar D G D G B D

"MY LADY E GWENDOLYN"

Arr. Pearse

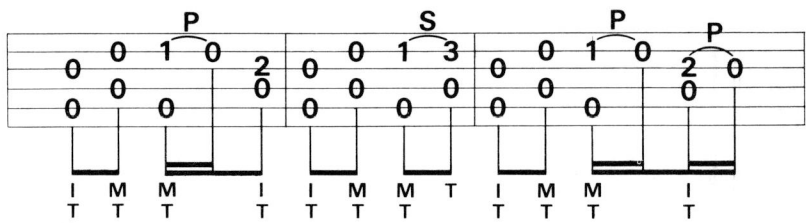

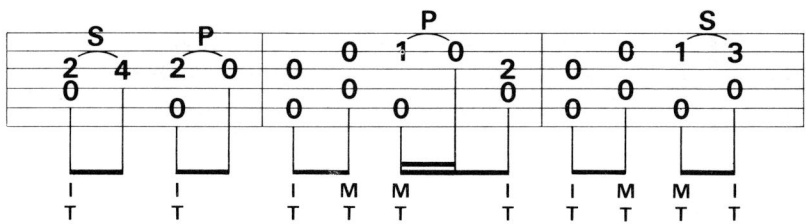

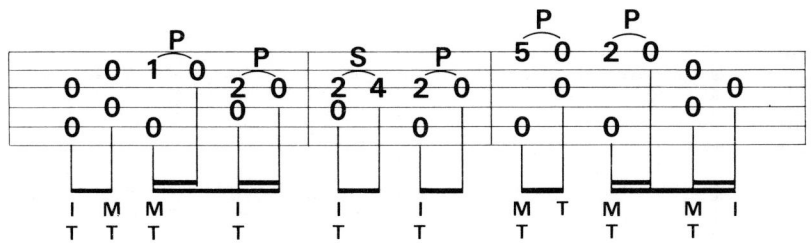

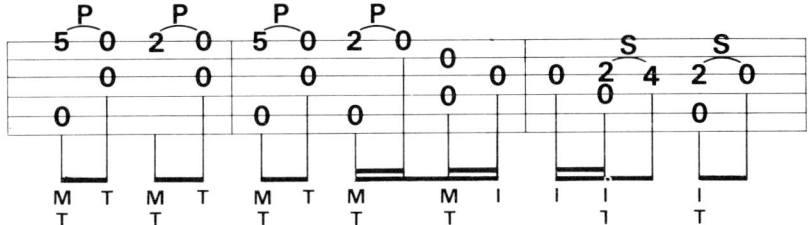

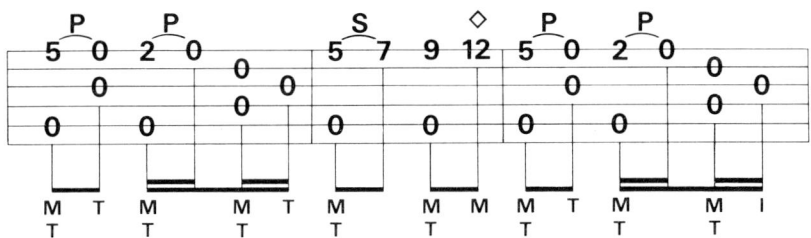

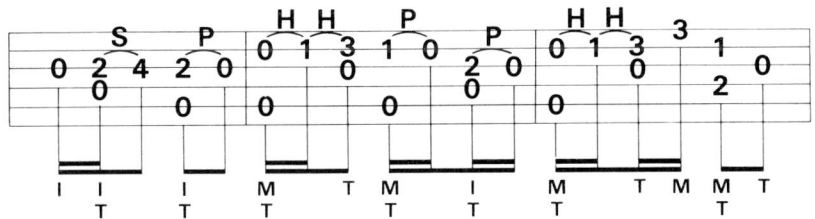

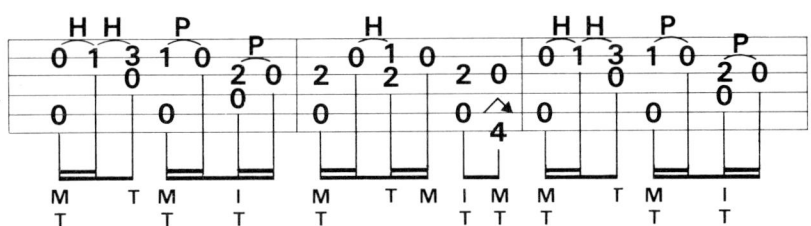

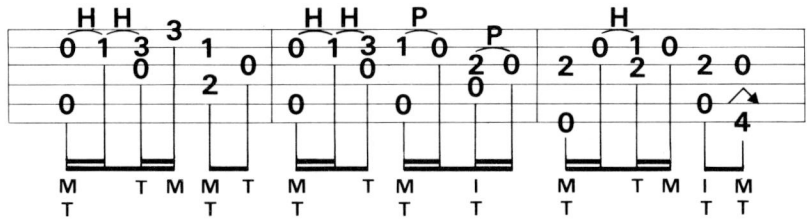

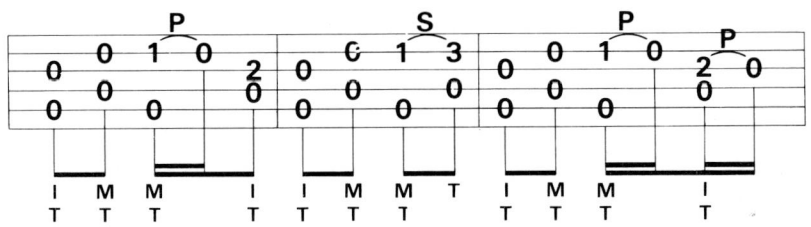

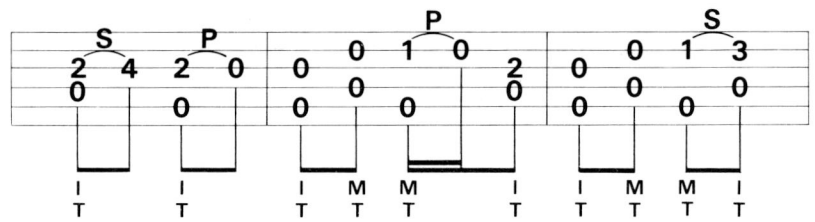

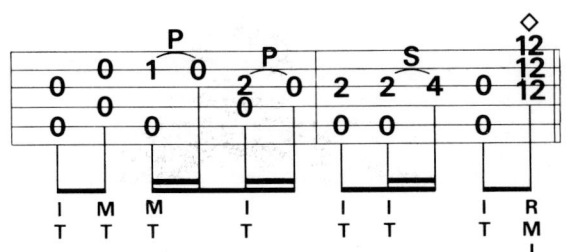

By the way, you'll see a couple of new signs in this tune. One occurs on the last note of BAR FOURTEEN:

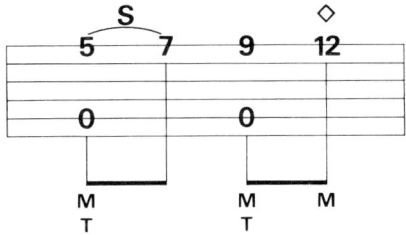

This diamond is the sign for a HARMONIC (what the French call a flageolet tone). A harmonic is the note that you get by touching a string at certain points along its length. This has the effect of changing its vibrating wave pattern. To go into the subject of harmonics would get us much deeper into music theory than I want to go in this book. But to give you some idea of how they work, imagine this to be our vibrating string:

You can see that the only two places which do not vibrate are those at either end of the string. We call these the NODES.

Now if you place a finger on the string at its exact center,

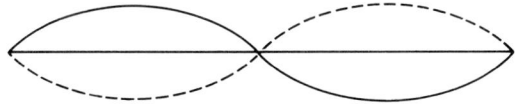

the string now vibrates in *two* exactly equal sections, because you've established a new node. As these two sections are each *half* the length of the original vibrating string, they each produce a note which is an *octave above* the original note. This is the effect that we want to achieve in "My Ladye Gwendolyne."

You can, if you want, use a finger to make a note at many different points on a string. One-third of the way along, for instance, causing the string to vibrate in *three* equal sections. This will produce yet another note, built up from the octave plus a fifth. But as I said, I don't want to get into music theory here. If you want to delve further, there are many fine books on the market that will lead you into this fascinating study.

So, now that you know a little about harmonics, let me show you how you play one on the guitar.

Look at BAR FOURTEEN again:

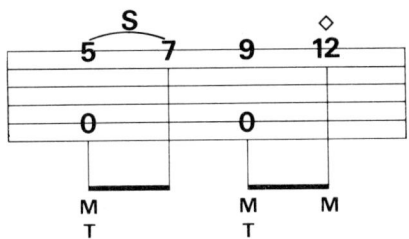

Touch the tip of a left-hand finger very gently onto the first string just over the twelfth fret. This is exactly halfway between the nut and the bridge saddle.

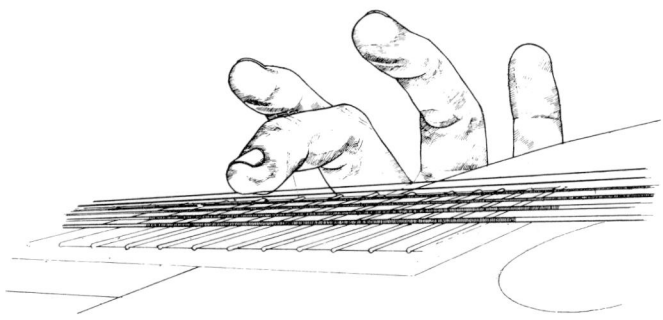

Now pluck the string with your right-hand middle finger and as the note rings out, remove your fingertip, allowing the harmonic to sing out clearly. If the note sounds "dead" or muffled, it could just be that you're pushing down too hard with your fingertip. The lighter, the better.

There are some more harmonics for you at the end of the last bar, BAR THIRTY-TWO:

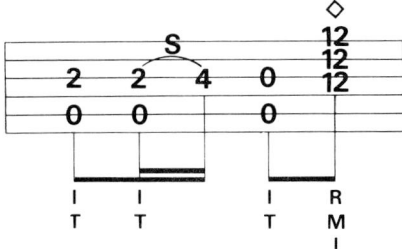

These are played by resting your finger, Barre fashion, across all four strings. This is slightly more difficult as you have to touch all the four strings just enough to produce the harmonic without killing the vibrations.

Now for the last new tablature sign, the sign for a BEND, or slurred note. It occurs first in BAR TWENTY:

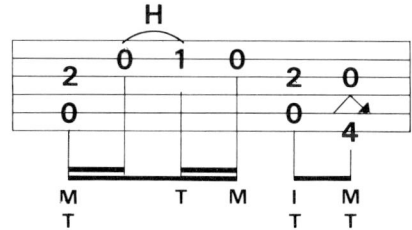

It just means that the fretted strings should be either pushed, or pulled, sideways on the fingerboard, causing the pitch of the string to rise up one halftone.

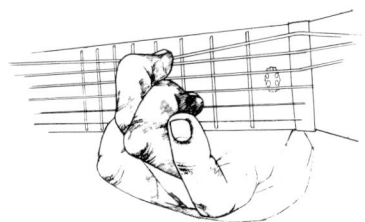

In this example the fretting finger pulls the string as it's ringing until the note glides up to that which would be produced were we to fret the string behind the fifth fret.

As I say, you can bend a string by either pushing or pulling it. However, if you pushed it in this instance, it would fall clear off the fingerboard, wouldn't it?

This device is used a great deal by blues and rock guitarists who, by using ultralight strings, can sometimes bend a string up two tones!

Occasionally you'll see tune tablature which has this arrow reversed:

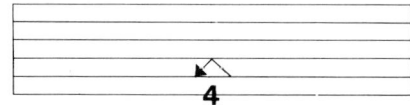

This just means that you should bend the string *before* you pluck it, then relax it down to the marked fret.

HAPPY PLAYING!

So here we are at the end of the book. No doubt there were times when you felt as though you'd never make it through. But you did. You now have the ability to play the guitar in a number of different styles, plus a basic performable repertoire. From here on it's up to you. Maybe you'll be content with just playing the pieces that I've shown you or maybe you'll go on, looking for new tunes and techniques. Maybe you'll even be tempted to take some people along with you, as I have done in this book. As I say, it's up to you. I've tried to unlock the door, but only you can walk through.

FRETBOARD DIAGRAM

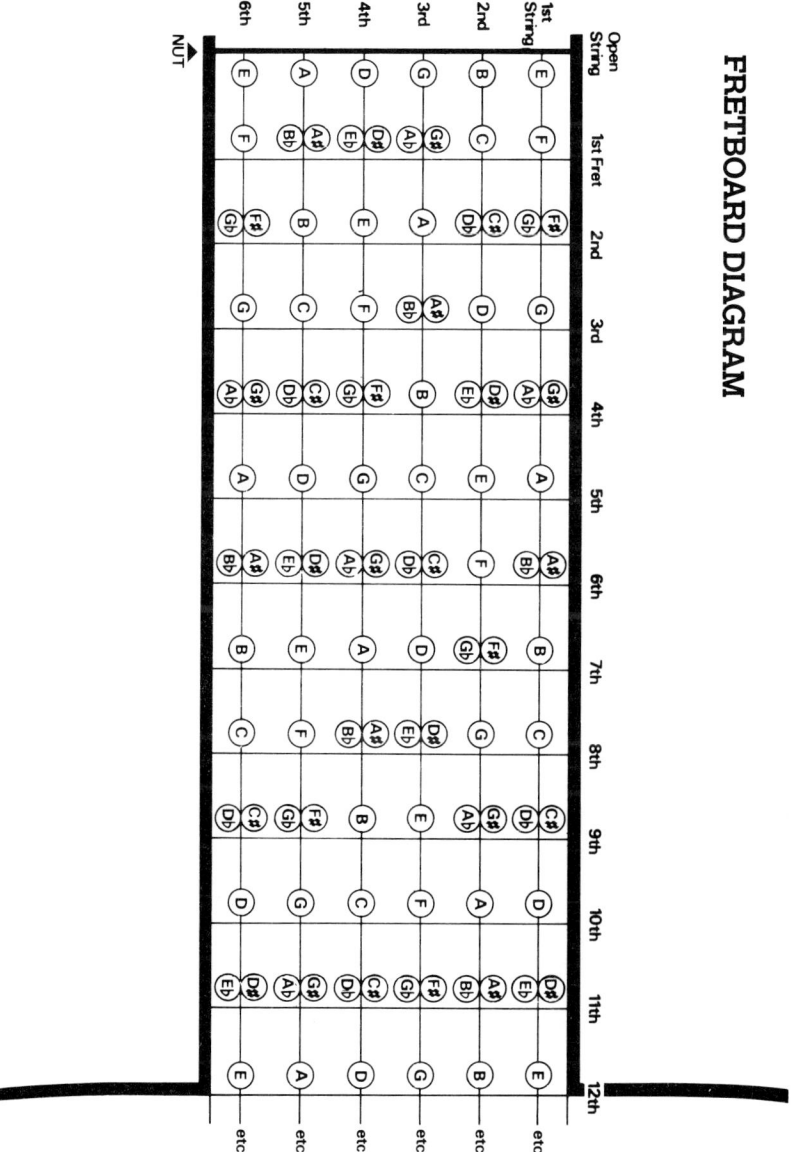

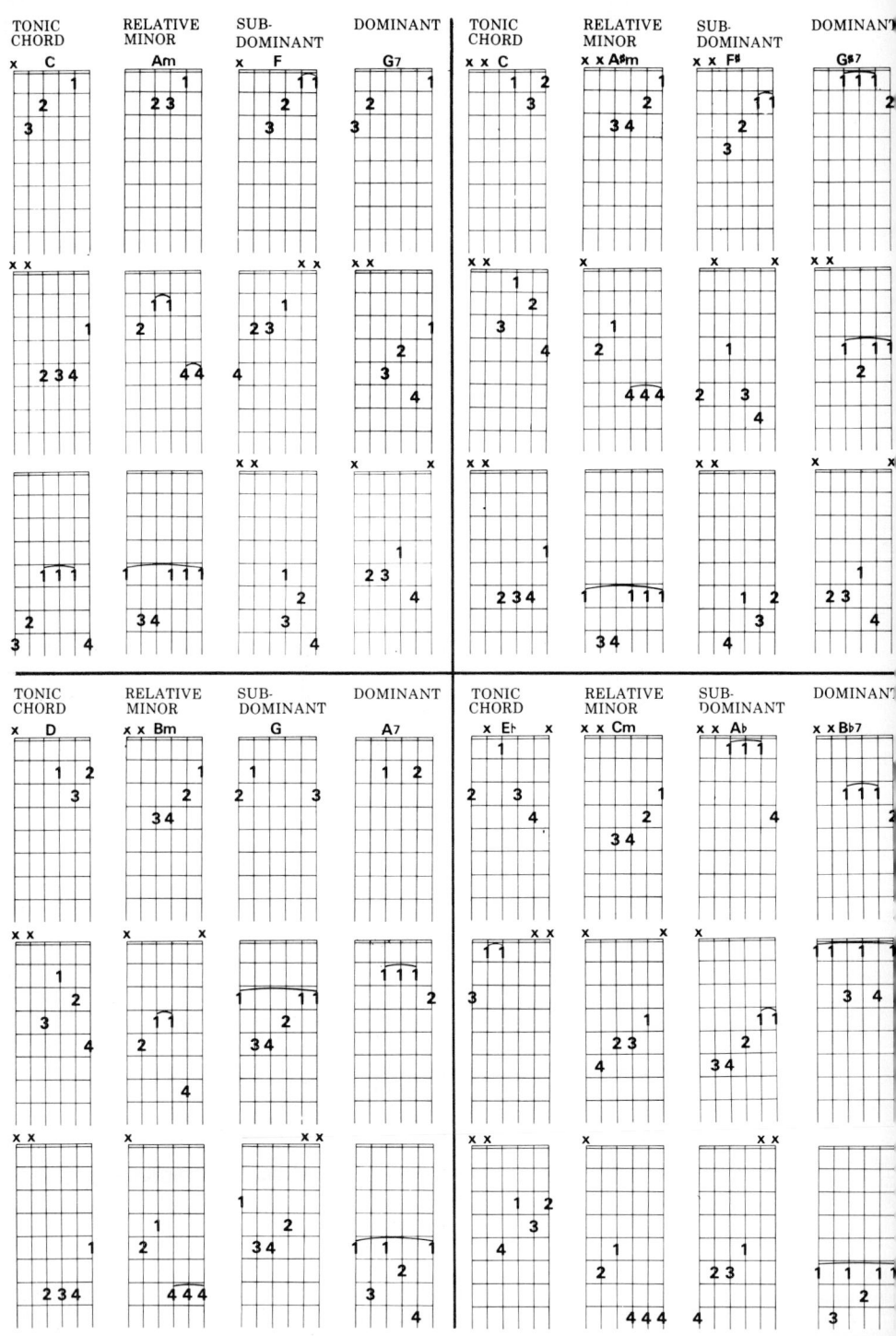

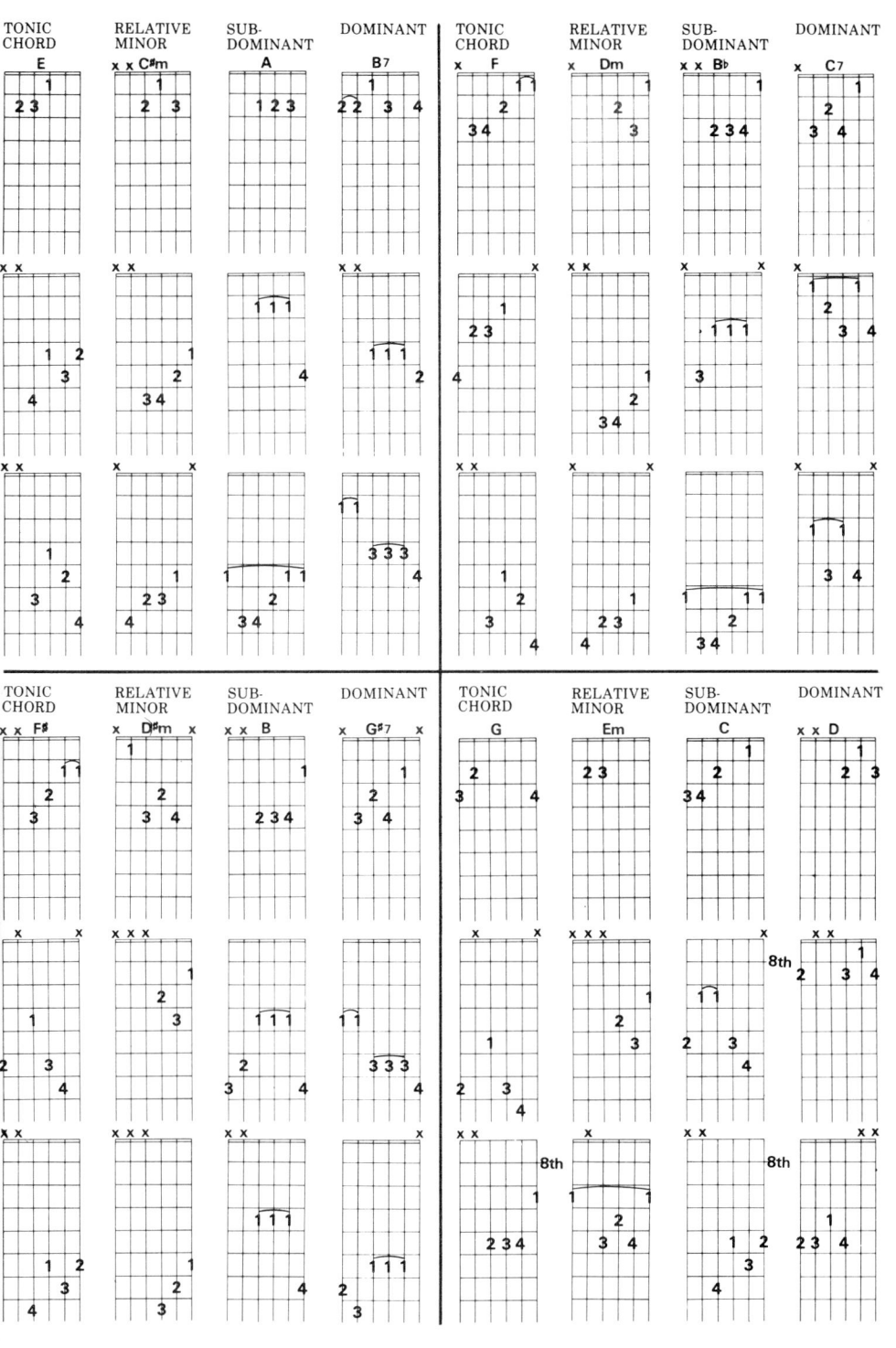

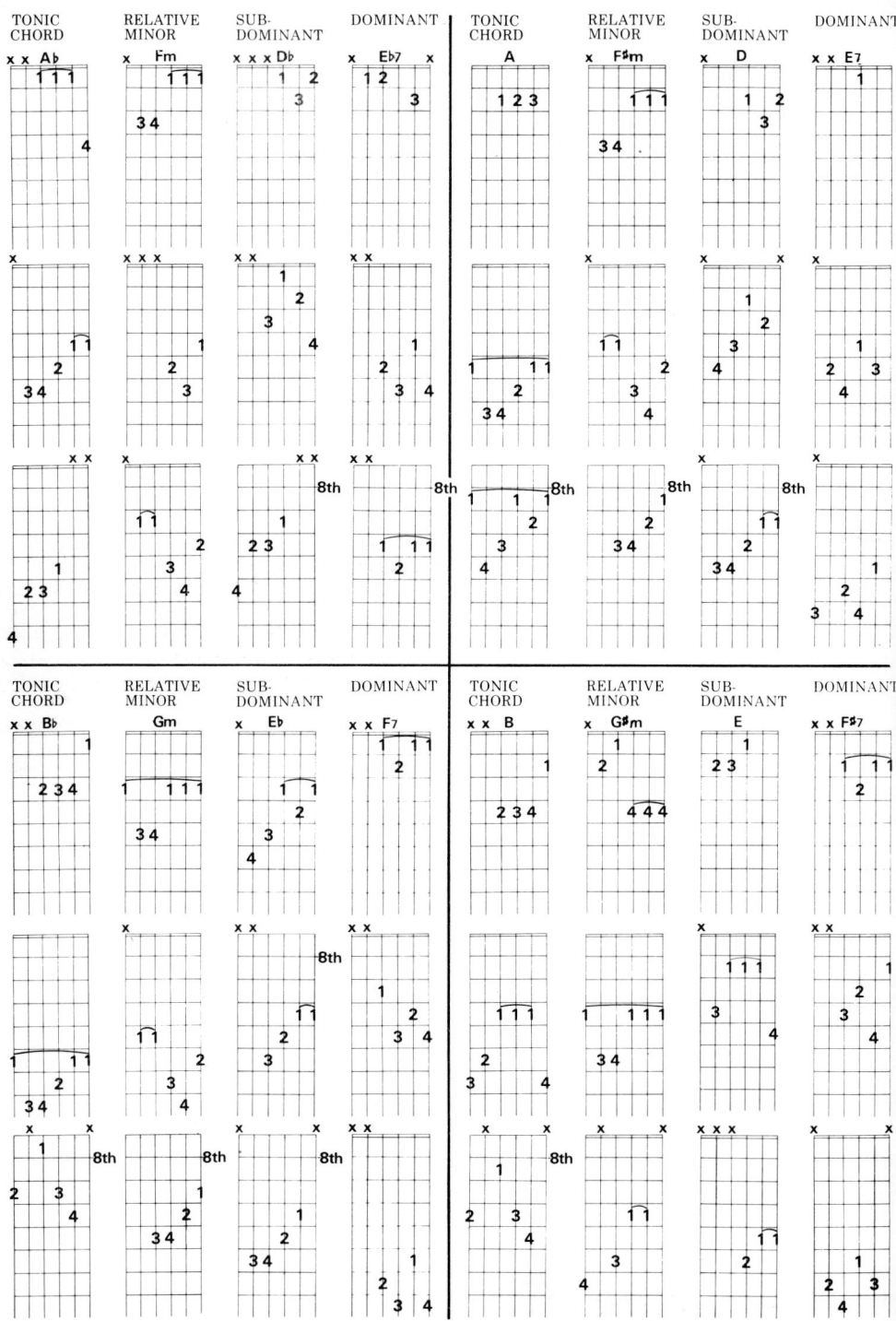